"The story of 10 Days of Prayer is one that I have had the privilege to watch unfold here in New England from the earliest days. When the vision is fully embraced, trumpeted and walked out, it inspires, motivates, and moves the church in a city or region forward together. This is what we have experienced in Connecticut. The 10 Days vision has catalyzed unity movements into reaching-the-city movements into let's-fulfill-the-Great-Commission movements. This book tells the initial story of one expression of the great End-Times ingathering that we are witnessing in our day. Read it and be inspired and motivated to join the movement."

Rick McKinniss
Wellspring Church

"As a Jewish believer in Yeshua/Jesus, the Feasts of the Lord have taken on a whole new meaning to me. I have found that our most precious Lord is at the very heart of each of them and that the Holy Spirit shows Himself through them in the most beautiful, unique ways to draw us closer to the heart of the Father. And none truer than the Ten Days of Awe, where now both believing Jews and Gentiles can come into a deeper place of reflection and repentance between Rosh Hashanah and Yom Kippur.

"I believe that the Father has designed 10 Days for this purpose and called Jonathan Friz to blow this holy shofar of mourning and repentance into these most wonderful days of prayer. What an incredible journey Jonathan has been on discovering these greater jewels in God's heart. This book tells the 10 Days story up until today. It is a must-read for all those seeking to go deeper with God. Seriously think about experiencing 10 Days of Prayer for yourself and your church or congregation. All aboard!"

Grant Berry
Founder, Reconnecting Ministries,
author and producer of *The Romans 911 Project*

"Jonathan Friz has been a dear friend since he took part in our ministry leaders' weekly prayer group in Santa Fe, New Mexico during his sojourn as a college student there about 20 years ago. In this book, he has a unique and wonderful story to share of how God so clearly called and enabled him to birth the 10 Days of Prayer movement. It has now spread to over 50 countries and 300 locations! The words of the song 'Amazing Grace' came to mind: '...through many dangers, toils and snares....' as I read through it. He recounts so many spiritual highs and agonizing lows that he and his patient, enduring wife Cassi, went through. It is truly an amazing, enthralling account, punctuated by much honest self-reflection and humorous asides, as Jonathan navigated so many mystifying ups and downs in his admirable determination to obey the original vision the Lord gave him.

"You will be captivated in reading about the Lord's great faithfulness and Jonathan's exemplary perseverance to guide such a valuable movement that is bringing unity and revival to His body across our world. Enjoy it!"

JOHN ROBB
Transformation Prayer Foundation
Unreached Peoples Task Force

10 DAYS

THE UNLIKELY STORY
OF A GLOBAL MOVEMENT
MOURNING FOR THE
RETURN OF JESUS

JONATHAN FRIZ

Published by Presence Pioneers Media, Farmville, NC
Cover design by Honour Fraiser.
Printed in the United States of America.

ISBN 978-1-951611-54-5 (print)
978-1-951611-55-2 (e-book)

DEDICATION

This book is dedicated with gratitude to my wife, Cassi.
Without your love, patience, and partnership this story
would not have been possible.
"Many daughters have done nobly, but you excel them all."

CONTENTS

INTRODUCTION

SINCE 2004, I have invited people around the world to stop everything and pray for 10 Days.

As you might imagine, that hasn't always gone over well.

Inspired by the ten-day upper room prayer meeting described in Acts 1 and by the Ten Days of Awe observed by the Jewish people for millennia, 10 Days is an annual invitation to take vacation time and enter into mourning, fasting, and repentance. It was sparked by a visionary experience in 2004, where I saw entire cities around the world stopped to worship Jesus.

10 Days has almost no paid staff, very little social media or marketing presence, no celebrity, and a tiny budget. The invitation to stop everything for ten days of mourning and repentance is unattractive and incomprehensible to most people. And yet, over almost twenty years, the movement has grown steadily and at times, suddenly. In 2023, 10 Days events took place in over 75 nations and 400 locations. In future years, we expect there will be even more united prayer events, many in some of the hardest and darkest corners of the world.

I've written this book to chronicle the history of the 10 Days movement, telling the story from early, formative experiences to the present moment (2023).

It's a story of miracles, divine guidance, and supernatural signs. It's about how prayer can affect cities and nations, the weather, an old campus, and even baseball. It's also a tale of foolish mistakes, bitter disappointments, being crushed, and what happens on the other side. It's about experiencing revival, the ways it can go wrong, and how it can be sustained. Ultimately, it's about the worthiness of Jesus Christ who is returning to earth to rule and reign, and how we have a part to play in the biggest wedding party in history.

This book is for the kids.

While I certainly have my own children in mind, I'm thinking of those who have already begun cultivating something special with God in secret, spiritual adventurers who have moved beyond dissatisfaction with the world and begun to actively seek out a better country. I'm writing as a father with you in mind, to encourage you not to give up, inspire your journey through some of my failures and mistakes, and also share some of what I've learned in the past twenty years.

If you've taken a step back in your walk with the Lord, I think this book will encourage you to get up, dust yourself off, and pick up where you left off.

And if you're intrigued by Jesus, but not sure what's described in the Bible is real (as I was), you may still enjoy this book. God is alive and real, but I hope you won't take my word for it. Seek Him out, and somehow find Him for yourself. While He often seems distant, He is not far from each one of us.

I've told these stories from memory aided by written records. I often consulted others who were involved to make sure details were correct. When I quote conversations between God and myself, they are usually from my personal prayer journal, although sometimes they are from memory. When stories are narrated where I was not present, they are taken directly from written or recorded first-hand accounts. I have no doubt that I may have misremembered minor details, but the major events all happened as told.

Some significant biblical ideas introduced in the book may be new to the reader. While I initially hoped to write theological sections to introduce major themes, it became clear I was writing a story, not a sermon. I'm hoping to write another book focused on key theological ideas for the praying church.

The story is told chronologically in two main sections.

For the seven years from 2004 to 2011, we attempted 10 Days in a variety of ways, from trying to spark a national movement, to small group gatherings, to retreats, to city-wide events. Because of how these formative experiences continue to shape the movement, I shared this part of the story in greater detail.

For those who are already doing 10 Days, the first section will be inspiring as you dream about what God could do in your own city. It shows different, significant ways God has moved through extended seasons of worship and prayer.

A major theme of the first section is how to have passion for God and walk in revival without hating everyone. I've tried to be candid about some of my failures and mistakes that caused great harm. Since that time, I've observed hundreds of other people making similar mistakes. People who are passionate for God miss the mark in ways that are consistent and repeatable. Hopefully, it will also be a reminder that God loves to work through foolish things.

The second section covers the years from 2012 to 2023. The main theme is the growth of the movement from just three locations in 2012 to over 400 in 2023. Many of the powerful God-encounters of the early days are experienced afresh by city-wide gatherings. One key sub-theme is how God loves to bring promotion through humility.

While the chapters are still chronological, they focus on just one or two key 10 Day gatherings from each year. Most of the incredible 10 Days gatherings that have taken place are not mentioned—there are simply too many. The same holds for the many miraculous stories we hear each year. As John 21 states, Jesus did too many miracles to fit them all in a book. I bear witness; He is still doing the same today. While I tried to be honest about my failures, many of those are also left out.

I hope this book will be a demonstration of the power of intensive, catalytic seasons of prayer to bring unusual spiritual growth, community transformation, and revival. If there's one thing that's clear to me, it's this: when we seek God, we find Him and when we pray more, God does more. In a world growing darker in many ways, these times of extraordinary prayer may no longer be optional for church life, they may be essential for us to make it with our faith intact in the days ahead.

While there are many incredible God stories told here, I'm convinced a much greater fullness is yet to come. After almost twenty years, we still haven't seen entire cities stop to worship and repent. Most people still don't get it.

And yet, whenever God's people come together to honor God the Father, exalt the Lamb who was slain, and turn away from sin, something amazing happens. The Holy Spirit unites us and fills our hearts with love for one another. God begins speaking, leading, driving us forward. Signs and wonders break out, new disciples are born, and the beauty of Heaven comes to Earth.

This is a story about mourning for the return of Jesus. Without a doubt, this is the major theme of 10 Days, that God's people would long, weep, and mourn for the return of His Son. My greatest hope and prayer for you is that these stories will fill your heart with expectation for His appearing. He is the rightful King of Heaven and Earth, who is coming quickly. Let's watch and wait for Him together.

Maranatha, Come Lord Jesus!

—Jonathan Friz
September 2023

PART ONE

FORMATION

1

ROAD TRIP (2004)

MARCH sunlight slid sideways into the bedroom, warming my face. It was Sunday morning. Before I was fully awake, I was aware of the presence of God in the room.

"This is not how I normally wake up," I thought with a smile.

The previous day I had driven a thousand miles from my college in Santa Fe to my hometown of St. Louis, Missouri. I was staying at a friend's home so I could surprise my dad on his fiftieth birthday. I was a senior in college and my final spring break had just begun. It was March 9, 2004.

Now, I was the one being surprised by my heavenly Father. The morning unfolded and an unusual sense of God's presence continued to hover around me.

As I climbed the steps of Central Presbyterian Church—a beautiful, gothic-revival stone structure— everything around me felt saturated in meaning and beauty.

I reached the top step and an usher handed me a bulletin. Under the influence of God's presence, this routine act of welcome felt deeply significant, as though I had been handed a personal message from God Himself.

Feeling inexplicable gratitude toward the usher, I looked down at the bulletin. The topic of the day's sermon was somehow...me. Or at least my biblical namesake, Jonathan.

"Then Jonathan made a covenant with David because he loved him as himself. Jonathan stripped himself of the robe that was on him, and gave it to David, with his armor, including his sword and his belt." 1 Samuel 18:3-4

"I feel like I'm in a movie," I thought as I took a seat near the front. I pinched myself several times to make sure this was not a dream.

As the pastor, Dr. Doriani, preached, he explained how weapons and clothing were typical objects exchanged in a binding covenant. What was unique about this passage was that in handing over his royal weapons, armor, and robe, Jonathan, who was the heir to Saul's throne, was acknowledging David as God's choice for king. Jonathan was the natural heir, but through this act, he laid down his right to kingship out of love for David and recognition of God's choice of David as king. He loved David so much he gave up his right to rule the kingdom.

As the sermon continued, I heard the Holy Spirit say to me: "You could be a king."

I understood—like Jonathan, by birth I had the gifts, the training, and the drive to succeed at whatever I set my mind to do in this life. I was about to graduate from college. I had considered law, and maybe even a career in politics. My entire future was before me.

"Will you strip off your robe, your armor, and your sword and give it to Me?"

In the moment, I didn't hesitate. All that I had, natural abilities, intelligence, ambition, seemed to me like filthy rags and less than nothing. Even if they brought enjoyment for a moment, I knew it was temporary.

I loved God's choice for king. It was a great joy to fully give my life to Jesus.

Soberly, I contemplated what this covenant had meant for Jonathan. He died a violent and premature death. He never was able to see the Davidic Kingdom. Would my path be similarly tragic? I had no idea what life would look like going forward. I did my best to wrestle with the possibilities, both bad and good.

As I left Central Presbyterian that morning, I knew that my course in life was set. My royal robes, my armor, my weapons, my right of self-determination was gone—everything now belonged to Him.

PERSONAL REVIVAL

It had always bothered me that while I was a Christian, my life looked nothing like lives of the people I read about in the Bible.

However, it seemed like that was starting to change. During the past year, I had been experiencing personal revival and getting to know the Holy Spirit in an entirely new way.

This new intimacy with God was sparked by an in-depth study of the gospel of John. As I dove into the fourth gospel, I was confronted with Jesus's words about the Holy Spirit in John 16:7:

"It is to your advantage that I go away; for if I do not go away, the Helper will not come to you; but if I go, I will send Him to you."

As I read this passage, I had two thoughts, one after the other:

"I do not believe this at all. I would much rather be able to talk to Jesus face-to-face than to have the Holy Spirit."

As soon as I honestly admitted this, a second thought immediately followed.

"I'm wrong and Jesus must be right. I need to get to know the Holy Spirit."

Somehow, I knew that the key to getting to know the Holy Spirit was having a strong prayer life, something I had never been able to do. As I began to pray consistently, clumsily in the winter of 2003, I began to see a change.

That summer, I encountered God's presence in a new and extraordinary way. Prayers were answered before my eyes, and minor miracles and wild coincidences happened around me with new regularity. I began to experience victory over besetting sin and freedom from the depression that had dogged me all my life. It was the beginning of my relationship with the Helper.

SEVEN DAYS DEVOTED TO PRAYER

Now, in March 2004, with the end of college fast approaching, I was sensing God calling me into ministry. While I sensed a general calling, I did not know what He wanted me to do specifically. I needed to hear from God, but I wasn't exactly sure how that was supposed to work. How does one hear from God?

The year before, my friend Glenn drove alone to North Dakota. For five days, he did nothing but pray, worship, and read the Bible. When he returned, he was transformed. He seemed closer to God than anyone I had ever met. He was holy; like someone who had stepped out of the pages of the Bible. His transformation made me jealous, in a good way. If God had done that for Glenn, He could do it for me.

Inspired by his journey, I decided to try something similar during spring break. First, I drove to my hometown of St. Louis, Missouri for my father's birthday celebration. From there, I planned to drive back to Santa Fe by way of Colorado, Montana, Oregon, and California, a journey of about 5,000 miles through the western United States.

My intention was to devote every waking hour of the seven-day journey to prayer, worship, listening to Scripture, and silent solitude.

I also planned to spend a few days fasting. To make the trip more interesting, I would avoid the main highways and take the backroads as much as possible. My wife Cassi somehow agreed to let me go on this adventure.

My hope for this seven-day road trip was summed up in a simple prayer:

"Lord, show me who I am and what you're calling me to do."

Years later, the memories are still vivid.

PRAYER JOURNEY

As I begin the journey west from St. Louis, the tangible presence of God surrounds me just as it did on Sunday. As I listen to the Scriptures, my heart is captured by passages like John 17:21, "Let them be one as We are one" and Psalm 133, "Behold how good and pleasant it is for brothers to dwell together in unity."

"Could it be God is calling me to a ministry focused on the unity of the church?" I wonder.

I have cared deeply about this issue for as long as I can remember. Now, I am beginning to suspect this passion is more than a childish fancy.

As I drive across Missouri, a strong desire fills my heart: For some reason, I want to see an oil painting at the church I attended as a child in a small farm town near Kansas City.

I remember certain things about the painting—it has three panels and hangs over the side entrance of the sanctuary—but for some reason I cannot remember what it portrays. I only know that I have to see it.

I exit the interstate, driving by memory on old roads I haven't seen since childhood.

I arrive at the white, country church just before sundown. The shadows are starting to lengthen. The sun is glimmering off the stained glass.

My mind is racing. "Is the door locked? Will I be able to get in to see the painting?"

A relieved gasp leaves my lips as the doorknob turns—in true rural fashion, the church is unlocked. I walk slowly down the aisle. The smell of the church is familiar. Each step unlocks a new childhood memory.

A PAINTING INTERPRETED

I reach the front of the Sanctuary, turn right, and look up. There is the oil painting in three panels—the mysterious object of my preoccupation.

It's a painting of the book of Acts, chapters one and two, the outpouring of the Holy Spirit on Pentecost.

In the first panel, the apostles and 120 first disciples are praying in the upper room, watching and waiting for the promise of the Holy Spirit.

In the second panel, flames of fire descend on the apostles. Peter is preaching while one of the apostles holds an inscription from Joel chapter 2: "I will pour out my spirit on all people."

The final section shows a great harvest of souls, with many baptisms.

As I stand, gazing in awe, I sense an interpretation.

There will be united prayer as there was in the upper room in Acts chapter 1. Then, there will be an outpouring of the Holy Spirit and revival, leading to a great harvest.

Could it be that God is answering me? Is He calling me to unite His church through prayer?

I am elated. My deep-seated desire for unity in the church, my fascination with the book of Acts, my longing for authentic Christian community; could it be that those deep longings are no accident but were put there by God Himself?

I leave the church as the sun drops below the horizon, my heart full of awe and wonder.

WHERE IS GOD?

As I hit the road, I am full of expectation for the remainder of the trip.

"This keeps going from glory to glory," I say to myself.

However, as the sun sets, things take a darker turn.

I leave the country church and God's presence evaporates. I don't understand. Even though all I am doing is praying, worshiping, and listening to the Bible, God's presence is gone. Like a hunter deep in the wilderness, my prey has vanished without a trace. I find myself alone, still in pursuit, in forbidding terrain.

I drive around 1,000 miles each day, first crossing Kansas, coming to the front range of the Rocky Mountains, and then heading north to Wyoming.

Meanwhile, in these days before GPS, the drive itself is anything but straightforward. March is a winter month in the Rockies and many of the backroads from Wyoming to Montana are closed due to snow. As one miserable day merges into the next, I find myself lost and lonely, realizing for the first time how meaningful even the slightest human interaction can be. The quest is beginning to feel like a complete failure.

WISDOM, MONTANA

After multiple dead-ends and hundreds of miles of backtracking, I finally make it to Montana and through the imposing Rockies. Despite all my efforts to pursue God, He remains elusive.

"I have completely wasted my time," I mutter, frustrated and discouraged.

My Rand-McNally Road Atlas shows a small town named Wisdom in the southwest corner of Montana near the border with Idaho.

On a whim, I head there from the interstate even though it is already very late. I want to get off the highways and back to the backroads. I am tired and need sleep. Wisdom is just an hour away.

Before long I find myself plunging up and down in the dark night over mountainous roads, hemmed in by mounds of snow. The pavement abruptly ends—the road is now red dirt and ice.

I am now miserable, entirely lost in the wilderness. Not a single electric light is visible. I find myself on an endless series of dirt roads bisecting a network of fields. For what seems like hours, I drive aimlessly, lost in a labyrinth with high snow walls that block my view. I pray my car keeps running and I don't get stuck or stranded. I could die out here in the cold. I have no idea if I am closer to Wisdom or further away.

Finally, I notice a light on the horizon. It looks like a farm or small industrial building. Wherever it is, it is the closest thing to civilization I have seen in a long time. As I come nearer to the light, I see a sign. I have reached Wisdom.

Wisdom Elementary School has been my lighthouse, drawing me safe to harbor. I pull into the parking lot exhausted, yet relieved, and immediately fall asleep in the car.

ON THE SALMON RIVER

As I awake in snow-covered Wisdom, my own barrenness stares me in the face. All my seeking and searching for God has produced nothing; God seems further away than when I started. And yet, with the sunrise, a glimmer of hope. Surely God is a rewarder of those who diligently seek Him.

"Let's keep playing this out," I think to myself.

Having driven more than 2,000 miles already, I decide to spend the better part of the day walking and praying. I discover a hiking and skiing area, fittingly called "Lost Trail" on the Idaho/Montana border.

But, after hours of walking through deep drifts of snow, I am just as frustrated, just as barren, and just as lost.

"Is God even real? Does He even exist?"

This is beginning to look more and more like a wild goose chase.

Reluctantly, I leave Montana and enter Idaho.

Idaho had always struck me as one of the least remarkable states. Now, as I drive into Idaho for the first time, on a serpentine road mirroring the Salmon River, I find myself in one of the most beautiful, desolate places I've ever seen.

The unexpected beauty of Idaho seems to open a door to the presence of God. As I enter a burned-out forest, devastated by wildfire, my dry and lifeless prayers are suddenly dynamic and alive.

On the inside, I'm like this forest. I'm burned and barren. God, would you send your rain to revive me again? A clean and godly mourning overflows. Tears erupt from deep within. I can't put the stopper back in the bottle. I have finally found God again, or more precisely, He has found me. I am overjoyed and yet, afraid because of the intensity of what is happening.

There, beside the Salmon River in Idaho, I experience my own personal outpouring of the Holy Spirit.

The beautiful sense of God's nearness and presence continues at varying levels of intensity for the remainder of the trip. As I make my way out of Idaho, through the stunning Columbia River valley, and down into California, I know I have found what I was looking for—God has called me to unite His people in prayer.

AFTERMATH

After seven days on the road, traversing more than 5,000 miles, I returned to Santa Fe a changed man.

As a skeptical, intellectual person, I often struggled to believe what I read in the Bible.

However, after countless hours of listening to Scripture, the Word of God began to come alive in a new way. Having this type of spiritual experience with the Scriptures made me realize the truth—the Bible is really inspired by God. This experience created a deep loyalty in my heart to God's Word, and faith that it can be trusted even when I don't understand.

With my new mindset, I began to have deeper insights into the Bible than in my more "intellectual" days. Different things that I had always wondered about in the Bible began to make sense. Passages about the Lord's return seemed especially powerful and I found myself growing in anticipation of His coming.

Spending long periods of time in prayer felt good. I felt clean, happy, and hopeful, as though my life was and would be meaningful.

RAPID GROWTH RINGS

After my experience on the Salmon River, I began hearing God's voice more clearly than ever before. Just as I had been unable to hear Him or sense His presence, after this experience, it was hard to turn it off.

At one point on my drive, I saw a cross-section of a tree in my mind's eye. The growth rings of the tree, each representing a year, were highlighted to me. As I saw this, I heard the inner voice of the Spirit interpret what I was seeing. "You've added several rings in just a few days." God was saying that somehow, spiritual growth that would normally take years could be condensed into much shorter periods of time.

"What would it be like if more Christians could experience these seasons of intensive spiritual growth?" I wondered.

Most importantly, I came out of my travels with a clear sense of calling, and the beginnings of the faith I would need to step into it.

I knew beyond a shadow of a doubt that God was calling me to work for the unity of His church. Jesus's prayer in John 17, "Let them be one as we are one," was ringing in my ears.

I also knew that God was calling me to pursue that unity of the Spirit through prayer. As in the Upper Room and as on that very trip, a time of waiting in prayer would precede the outpouring of the Spirit. Expectation for unprecedented, global revival and hundreds of millions coming to Jesus filled my heart.

And finally, I was convinced that all these elements—extraordinary prayer, supernatural unity, revival, and a great harvest—were all somehow related to what would happen on earth before the Lord's return. My new experiences with God filled me with expectation for the return of Jesus Christ.

2

PRAYER NET (2004)

IN APRIL of 2004, shortly after my return to Santa Fe, a recurring image kept coming into my mind.

The image was of a rectangular net composed of red light. Or rather, the strands of the net seemed to be light, while the connection points seemed more solid. I'd see this image whenever I let my mind wander or when I prayed. Sometimes, it was accompanied by a sense of God's peaceful presence. I started asking a question that was strange to me at the time.

"Is this image in my head God trying to speak to me?"

Some might believe it is crazy to think that an image in your mind is God talking to you. Others may see it as completely normal. I was somewhere between those two positions. The Bible had convinced me the Holy Spirit wanted to speak to me, and I had several experiences where I was confident God had talked to me. However, it wasn't normal and I was still trying to figure out how to hear His voice. Despite my inexperience, I couldn't shake the sense that this picture in my imagination seemed to be from God.

As I meditated on the image, an interpretation started to form.

"I think the cords of the net made of red light are prayers and the connection points are churches," I mused.

"God, are you asking me to start a net of prayer to unite the church?"

TERROR PARALYSIS

A conviction was growing in my heart: God wanted me to start a prayer network in Santa Fe, something that would unite the churches of the city. There was one big problem. I was terrified.

While I was afraid to step out and obey, the picture God had showed me burned inside me, like steam in a kettle that was beginning to boil. For the first time, I understood what the prophets meant when they described God's word as fire in their bones. I felt as though if I didn't do something, I would explode. At the same time, I was paralyzed by fear. Something had to give.

I called a good friend and mentor to talk over the situation. I hemmed, hawed, and complained, explaining all the reasons I wasn't doing what God had showed me. He saw right through the smoke-screen.

"If God is calling you to do this, stop being a coward, stop complaining, stop making excuses, and go do it. Besides, He's probably already shown you where to start."

The rebuke hurt, but I knew he was right. Like a slap in the face, the pain brought instant clarity. I realized I did know where to start—in fact I had known all along but fear had blinded me.

PASTOR JIM

The next day, I showed up unannounced at Capital Christian Church, a large, centrally located congregation in the city. I was terrified.

"What am I doing here?" I mumbled as I forced myself to take one tormented step, then another, then another.

Haltingly, I spoke to the receptionist.

"Can I speak to the pastor?"

"He is away today, but perhaps you could speak to the associate. Can I tell him what you'd like to talk about?" she answered.

What was I there to talk about? How had she managed to ask me the most difficult question ever devised? Stumbling over my words, I managed something resembling a reply.

"I want to...unite the churches of Santa Fe...prayer."

Forming complete sentences was a lost cause.

"Okay, let me see if pastor Jim is free to talk with you." She was as kind and normal as I was awkward.

When the associate pastor finally invited me into his office, I was so afraid I was visibly shaking. He asked me why I was there.

"Unity...Prayer..." I barely managed to get two words out.

As I stood in front of his desk trembling, pastor Jim got out of his seat, approached me, and put a hand on my shoulder.

"Son, it sounds like you've been hearing from God. Let's go sit somewhere where we'll be more comfortable."

His kind words broke the spell. As we sat, my tongue was loosed, and I shared the vision of a prayer network to unite the churches of Santa Fe. I told pastor Jim my plan: I wanted to visit each church and ask a simple question, "Would you be willing to pray for three other churches each week during your Sunday service?"

Jim seemed genuinely encouraged by our conversation and invited me to join the weekly pastor's fellowship that met at Capital Christian. Somehow, I had stumbled into the hub of Christian unity in the city of Santa Fe. My fearful first step of faith was already bearing good fruit.

SUMMER ON MISSION

In May of 2004, I graduated from college. That summer, I was on a mission from God. Armed with a telephone and a yellow phone book, I made cold-call after cold-call and set up meetings with Christian leaders throughout the city. After my initial meeting with Pastor Jim, I would go on to visit a total of forty-nine different pastors and priests in the city. I had meetings with almost all the historically Christian denominations, including Roman Catholic, Eastern Orthodox, mainline Protestant, Pentecostal, Charismatic, fundamental Baptist, and pretty much everything in-between.

The meetings with church leaders ranged from instant brotherhood that defied explanation to open hostility. Some saw my presence as a sign that God was at work, others viewed me as an annoyance to be swept out the door as quickly as possible. The problem for the reluctant and annoyed ministers was, I was extremely persistent. And it was hard to argue with the biblical mandate to love and pray for one another. Sometimes, I'd drive away rejoicing, other times I'd want to cry because of their hurtful words. Some of these Christians were mean!

AN INTRODUCTION TO 24/7 PRAYER

The weekly pastor's fellowship at Capital was an oasis for me. It was incredible to be able to spend time with seasoned pastors who shared my passion for unity in the body of Christ and revival. One of the members of the fellowship was John Robb, founder of the International Prayer Council and, at the time, global prayer director for World Vision.

John gave me a book by an Englishman named Pete Grieg titled Red Moon Rising. The book was about a 24-7 prayer movement that started in England in 1999.

This movement of young people was inspired by a small group of immigrants in Hernhut, Germany called the Moravians. In the summer of 1727, they began a prayer meeting that continued twenty-four hours a day, seven days a week for over a hundred years. The fruit of this incredible 100-year prayer meeting was a missions movement that touched the ends of the earth. Somehow, this tiny community of about 600 believers in the middle of nowhere had started the Protestant missions movement.

Pete's story seemed a lot like mine—a normal believer who started praying, and then found himself involved in a God story seemingly ripped from the pages of the New Testament. I was starting to realize that the strange and unique experiences I was having were part of something much larger than me, something happening around the globe.

The title, Red Moon Rising, referred to Joel chapter 2 and the prophetic promise that the "moon would turn to blood" before the return of the Lord. Like me, Pete had a sense that our prayers were somehow connected to the Lord's return. Could it be that we would be part of the generation that would see Jesus's return?

I finished Red Moon Rising in my car before a meeting. It was dark outside, so I had to use the weak lights in my old car to finish the book, but I was totally engrossed and couldn't put it down. As I read the last words and stepped out of the car, I looked up. Shining brightly in the night sky was a full moon, glowing red as a barn door. It was the first "red moon" I'd ever seen in my life. Not brown, not orange, not yellow—blood red. I couldn't believe my eyes.

JOHN 17

During this season and ever since, Jesus's prayer in John 17 "Let them be one as We [the Father and the Son] are one," has been my driving motivation.

John chapter 17 is the longest prayer of Jesus recorded in the Bible. In the prayer, He repeats the main theme of His prayer three times, that His future followers would be one.

If Jesus were simply praying for unity among His followers, we would understand that this was a strong value for Him and key to our life as followers of Christ. Leaders from all walks of life want their followers to be united. There's nothing unusual about that.

It's how Jesus wants us to be one that makes the prayer so unbelievable.

"Let them be one just as We [the Father and the Son] are one."

Jesus wants His followers to be one "just as" God the Father is one with God the Son. He wants us to be one as God is one with God. This should not be possible.

And yet, Jesus boldly prays this prayer for His disciples on earth in the midst of the sinful world.

THE MESSIAH'S DYING WISH

Keep in mind the context of John 17—within twelve hours of praying this prayer, Jesus would be hung on a cross. Shortly after, He would die. His prayer in John 17 is His dying wish to the Father.

As we confront the impossible reality of what Jesus is praying for, we are left with several unavoidable conclusions.

First, Jesus is clearly praying for His disciples here and now, in this present age, not for people in Heaven or after He returns. He's praying for the church living in the world.

According to our lived experience, Jesus's prayer is impossible—we know people cannot be one as God is one with God. We've never seen the fullness of this prayer answered, either in our own experience or in history.

At the same time, can we imagine a scenario where the Father doesn't answer Jesus's prayer? Can we imagine the Father ignoring the dying wish of His beloved Son? I don't think so.

The Father is going to answer Jesus's prayer—we are going to be "one as the Father and Son are one so that the world may know that You sent me, and have loved them just as you loved Me." (John 17:23) Jesus's prayer is prophetic. It points to where we are going because the Father won't forget and can't resist the dying wish of His Son.

FROM VISION TO REALITY

As the summer wound down, I set the first Sunday in September as the launch date of the new Santa Fe Prayer Net. Of the forty-nine churches I visited in the city, thirty-nine had agreed to be part of the prayer network and pray for three other congregations in the city each Sunday. I printed off and hand-delivered materials to every church. Incredibly, God had faithfully led me from seeing a "picture in my mind" to actually seeing the vision come to pass.

And as the Santa Fe Prayer Net launched, I knew I had done something small but significant to make Jesus's prayer a reality. I had no idea how God was going to pull it off, but I was full of faith that the Father was going to answer Jesus's prayer—the church was going to be one, "just as [the Father and the Son] are one."

3

THE 10 DAYS VISION (2004)

WORKING FOR GOD

THE Santa Fe Prayer Net was a revelation. I had heard from God, stepped out in faith, and now what God showed me in a vision was happening in the real world. Now, thirty-nine congregations in Santa Fe were praying for one another on a weekly basis.

As the Prayer Net launched, I had a realization—"I work for God." I had finally figured out what I wanted to do when I grew up. Working for the Lord was challenging, exhilarating, terrifying, liberating, and satisfying. Why would I ever want to do anything else?

I did have a question: How does someone who works for God figure out what to do next? If I had an earthly boss, I would just ask him, "What do you want me to do?" How could I pose that same question to the Lord?

As I searched the Scriptures with this question in mind, I came across Daniel chapter ten. In this passage, Daniel eats "no pleasant food, no meat, or wine" for three weeks. After the twenty-one days of fasting are finished, Daniel has an encounter with an angel that brings him revelation about the end of the age.

"Daniel worked for God, like me," I reasoned. So why not try what Daniel did? As I entered this season of fasting in late August 2004, I had two questions for God.

"What do you want me to do next?" and "How can I be part of seeing Jesus get the answer to His prayer in John 17?"

Most Christians I spoke to didn't think Jesus's prayer would ever be answered—it was this incredible secret hiding in plain sight right there in the Bible. But I knew, and I was asking my new Boss what the next step was towards its fulfillment.

"YOU ARE THE PROBLEM"

Coming off an amazing summer, I was riding high and walking closely with God almost constantly. I could sense His nearness every day, whether I was taking a long evening prayer walk, working at my restaurant job, or spending time with friends.

However, as I entered this twenty-one-day fast, it felt as though God's hand lifted off me. Prayer became much less enjoyable, and I struggled to experience God's presence or hear His voice.

"Is this normal?" I wondered. "I thought the fast was supposed to help me hear from God."

In the first week of the fast, I accepted an invitation from John Robb to attend a gathering of New Mexico prayer leaders at the Glorieta retreat center in the Pecos Mountains. While there, I found myself in an unfamiliar setting. This was a gathering of "prophetic people" who were all hearing from the Lord and sharing what God was saying to them all the time. While I had grown in my respect for Charismatics over the past year, this was overwhelming and very strange. I was the youngest person there by at least twenty years.

Simply put, these old people were not cool. Their super spiritual style was incredibly off-putting. And many of these weird prophetic people were visibly arrogant and puffed up. In my heart, I knew I would much rather spend time with my unbelieving friends from college, who were interesting, intelligent, and understood me better.

After returning from the event and mulling over what I had seen, I heard the Lord speak to me. It was the first time I had heard Him clearly during the fast.

"Do you know why Jesus's prayer in John 17 is not being answered?" He asked.

"No," I answered truthfully.

"YOU are the problem."

It felt as though an enormous finger landed squarely on my chest. Immediately, I knew I was guilty as charged. Here I was, fasting and praying for an answer to Jesus's prayer. Meanwhile, in the middle of that fast, I was judging my own brothers and sisters. I looked down on them because they were old, weird, immature, and worst of all, not cool. To further my guilt, I even loved my unbelieving friends more than my own family, fellow followers of Jesus. This was not what the Lord had taught us to do at all—He told us to "love one another [fellow believers] as I have loved you."

The Lord had showed me what was keeping Him from answering Jesus's prayer. It was me.

I did not like being rebuked by the Lord—it hurt! I wanted to avoid that rebuke in the future as much as possible. Coming out of this experience, I made a commitment to love and honor every brother and sister in Christ that I met, regardless of any other factors. Some of us are weird and some normal, some are old and some young, some are cool and others are anything but. We have people who are mature and kind, and others who are immature and puffed up. However, for me the words of Jesus were ringing: "love one another, as I have loved you."

A STRONG TEMPTATION

As the fast continued, it seemed like God was keeping His distance. I persevered in times of prayer and especially in reading the Scriptures, but everything was dry and laborious.

As this spiritual dryness persisted, I began to have a very strong, recurring thought. Perhaps I had missed God's best for my life by getting married. After all, Paul says that it's better to remain unmarried so we can serve the Lord wholeheartedly. Could it be that God was calling me to leave my wife and become a traveling monk, going from place to place preaching the gospel and living off whatever people gave me, like a modern-day St. Francis?

The idea was upsetting—but what if it was God? I shared it with my wife, and for obvious reasons, she thought it was a bad idea. I thought it was a bad idea. But what if it was a "God idea," something He wanted me to do, like Abraham putting Isaac on the altar? I had to be ready to do anything, to make any sacrifice. Nevertheless, the thought troubled and tormented me, while also appealing to a part of me that wanted to be free to roam around without anything or anyone holding me down.

As the end of the fast grew near, God's presence was a distant memory. Looming on the horizon was the question of what I should do next.

"Should I jump at this wandering monk idea?" I wondered. It was the best next move I had. The "Net of Prayer" vision had worked out. Maybe this was the next step?

I was beginning to get desperate. The entire fast felt like a failure. I felt like a failure. Why was God so far away? Why wouldn't He speak? Everything depended on His voice.

"YOU'RE BACK"

On the twentieth night of the fast, as I prayed, God's presence returned. I said out loud, "You're back" as I sensed His warm, peaceful presence. I sat quietly, crying with relief and listening as He began to speak.

"Put the idea of leaving your wife out of your mind," He said. "That is not from Me."

Although I was so terribly wrong on the matter, it was not a harsh rebuke, just gentle, warm, and matter of fact.

What a relief to hear those words! And what a lesson on what the voice of the enemy sounds and feels like. Years later, I would learn that several famous saints had done exactly what I was tempted to do—left their husbands, wives, and families to pursue a seemingly more spiritual path. It seems I was not the first person the enemy tried to pull that trick on.

I continued to hear the Lord: "I want you to pray daily for the churches [of Santa Fe] at the Cathedral downtown. There is a specific place there that I want you to pray—I will show it to you."

My prayer time concluded, full of sweetness and beauty. God's presence had returned and I had heard His voice. It wasn't what I was ultimately looking for, but He was back.

A LONG WALK

Anticipation was building as I entered the last night of the fast. As the sun began to set, I headed out on what would be a long and eventful walk. I found I prayed and listened better when I was walking. At the time, it was normal for me to disappear for a few hours each evening to walk and pray with the Lord. If Adam had cool twilights in the garden, I had late nights in the high desert.

As I started walking, questions dripped one-by-one into my mind:

"What if this doesn't work?"

"What if God doesn't talk to me?"

"Maybe I'll just keep fasting until I find what I'm after."

Before I could worry too much, God started speaking.

His voice resounded in me: "You are someone who goes before someone greater to prepare a way for them."

I peppered the Lord with questions.

"Who is this greater one? Am I preparing for the return of Jesus? Or do you mean a younger person who will be greater? Or do you mean the next generation?"

I received no response to these questions. Instead, the Lord continued speaking about what my ministry would look like, giving me four biblical examples.

"You will be like Moses before Joshua, like Jonathan before David, like Elijah before Elisha, and like John the Baptist before Jesus."

My mind flooded with thoughts that I'll try to untangle and relate as best I can.

I felt relieved and excited—God was speaking after a long silence. The Daniel 10 fast was working. And who knew what He was about to say next? Everything could change in an instant.

"What He is saying makes sense of so many other things in my life," I thought.

Jeremiah chapter 1 speaks of how God called the prophet before he was even born. I was beginning to understand that word in a new light. The circumstances of my birth, things spoken by my parents, desires and questions that had always been inside of me—it felt as though everything finally made sense in light of this word from the Lord.

With this new understanding of what God had called me to do was an understanding of why I often felt like I didn't fit in.

I realized, "I don't fit in because God has made and called me to do something different, something I didn't even know existed. And now I understand more clearly what that is."

A final thread of thought was more forward looking.

"God, this is amazing, but it still doesn't answer my bigger question at all—'What do you want me to do?'"

After this initial experience, which lasted about twenty minutes, I heard nothing from the Lord for several hours.

The fact is, I was holding out for God to speak to me through an angelic encounter, just as He had spoken to Daniel. Part of the motivation without a doubt was to see something amazing that would convince both me and others that I had heard from God. Undoubtably, there were deeper insecurities and unbelief, mixed with a genuine desire to hear from God that contributed to this demand. In hindsight, I had no idea what I was asking, considering the angel was so terrifying Daniel couldn't move without help.

I was so insistent on this with the Lord that I vowed to keep walking and praying until I had an angelic encounter. So, I did. For three hours. By that point, I was wiped out and decided to head home in defeat. I clearly didn't have the staying power to follow through on my overzealous commitments. A bit of walking around and I was ready to throw in the towel. Often, our zeal that seems "spiritual" is counterproductive to what God wants to do by grace.

THE VISION

Finally, in desperation I removed this requirement of the Lord.

"Lord, I don't care how you speak to me. I don't need to see an angel, just tell me what to do."

As had happened on my long trek across the country, what began in a powerful encounter had dried up, and God seemed distant. However, He was simply waiting for me to get over myself so He could speak words and release vision that would change my life and impact people around the globe.

As I walked home, now open to even the crumbs from God's table, I felt somewhat dejected. This hadn't worked out as I had hoped. I was admitting defeat, walking back.

Santa Fe is in the high desert, a small city of 60,000 people surrounded by empty wilderness. The clear night air was refreshingly cool and dry as I walked. The sky was full of stars and you could see the Milky Way clearly above. In an open lot to my left sat a couple of concrete handball courts. I sometimes liked to stop there and sing my prayers at night, but this night I was tired and prayed out. As I passed by the courts, I suddenly felt the presence of God and heard a phrase in my spirit:

"Babylon refuses to mourn."

In hindsight, I would ponder how strange and mysterious the phrase was. In the moment, I was struck by the suddenness of God speaking to me. It was like hearing someone talk to you out of the blue when you think you're alone. I felt the nearness of God, but I was also afraid. I was suddenly in the presence of someone very great and powerful. I stopped walking and turned around as if a physical person were speaking to me, even though I knew I was hearing the words internally. As I stopped, I felt a response well up within me.

I answered: "But Your people will mourn before You return."

As I pondered this exchange, I understood it immediately. If Babylon, the kingdom that opposes God, is characterized in Revelation chapter 18 by a refusal to mourn, resulting in ultimate judgment when Jesus returns, it made sense that God's people would move in the opposite spirit, that they would mourn while the world rejoiced, and then rejoice when Babylon was mourning.

Also, I knew inside that THIS was the moment I had been seeking. After twenty-one days, I had my audience with the Boss.

It began to be very simple to speak and hear the Lord. I was able to ask him questions and hear clearly, much like a normal conversation.

"Lord, what is it that you want me to do?"

In response, I heard, "Call my people to 10 Days of fasting, mourning, and repentance from Rosh Hashanah to Yom Kippur."

Once again, this out-of-the-blue direction made perfect sense to me. I had studied the biblical feasts described in Leviticus 23, and I knew that the fall feasts had special prophetic significance related to the Lord's second coming. In Jesus's first coming, He fulfilled the feasts of Passover and Pentecost on the exact days. His sacrificial death was a fulfillment of Passover and the outpouring of the Spirit was a fulfillment of Pentecost. Could it be that something similar would happen with the fall feasts as well? I knew that there was a ten day period between the Day of Trumpets, also called Rosh Hashanah and the Day of Atonement or Yom Kippur. Could it be that as we approached the Lord's return, there would be a renewed emphasis in the Church on these fall feasts?

"Who is this for?" I asked. "Is it for Santa Fe?"

Instantly, I heard, "It's bigger."

And in my mind's eye I saw a map of New Mexico.

"Is it for New Mexico?"

"It's bigger," came the response, and the map zoomed out.

"Is it for the Southwest?"

"It's bigger."

And the map zoomed out. As it got bigger and bigger, I became more and more afraid. Eventually, the map was the size of the United States, and I yelled out loud "Stop." And so that part of the vision stopped.

"What have I gotten myself into?" I said to myself. I just wanted to know what God wanted me to do next, and somehow God was showing me something with national and even global implications.

Wondering how I could possibly do something on this scale, I asked, "How am I supposed to do this?"

Immediately, in my mind's eye, I saw myself driving around the country, meeting people one by one, and sharing face-to-face.

This image was comforting. I realized that what seemed enormous and beyond my control was as simple as having conversations, one by one, with other believers as I had done in setting up the Santa Fe Prayer Net.

Next, the vision shifted to a truly remarkable scene, a city completely covered by the glory of God.

I knew that this city had stopped everything. Normal life had been suspended for ten days of worship, prayer, fasting, and repentance. Businesses were closed, schools were closed, and shopping centers were empty as people gathered to humble themselves before God in one accord.

It was as though a city on earth had become a perfect representation of the throne room in Heaven, described in Revelation chapters four and five. This city was completely covered in what seemed to be a thick, golden cloud that surrounded it like a liquid surrounding a snowglobe. The presence of God was so thick it was difficult to see through. I knew this city would never be the same.

As I saw this, two questions bubbled up from within me.

"God, how would you respond if a city sought you in this way?"

"Is this how you want to answer Jesus's prayer in John 17?"

By now, I had returned home. Although Cassi and I lived in a community house with other residents, it was late, no one was awake, and the lights were all off. Although God had seemed distant for weeks and I hadn't heard anything from Him, now I found I couldn't turn the faucet off. God kept speaking as I sat down on the couch in the dark. We continued our conversation.

"You're also going to pray for ten days leading up to Pentecost this year," He said.

These words activated my sense of the absurd.

"Lord, I don't think anyone is going to believe me or listen to me as it is. I don't think anyone will 'stop everything' for 10 Days once a year, much less two times a year. God, this is too much 10 Days!"

Of course, this isn't what the Lord said. He had given me a specific instruction for the next year, 2005.

By this point, I was feeling every emotion at once—fear and fright, excitement, joy, fear again, wonder, joy again, all swimming in an ongoing and powerful sense of God's presence.

As we continued our conversation that night, God spoke to me about several other things. At the time, the experience was so intense I thought I would never forget a single detail. I didn't even write it down that night, although I would do a lot of writing about it over the next months. I had never been trained on how to steward God's words, so I didn't know I needed to write it down. Some of the further details of what happened I can no longer remember in detail. Thankfully, the points I've shared here are just as strong, largely because I've shared them thousands of times since.

As I went to bed, I was elated. Before falling asleep, I shared briefly with Cassi that I had heard from the Lord.

One way or another, I understood that what had just happened would change everything about my life going forward.

As I fell asleep, questions lingered in my mind:

"What will life be like tomorrow?"

"What kind of person am I becoming?"

And most pressingly, "What have I gotten myself into?"

4

CONFIRMATION (2004)

As I awoke the next morning, I was full of joy. God had spoken to me. The Daniel 10 fast had worked. Also, that evening I would finally break the fast—always a cause for celebration.

I looked at the calendar to see when the Day of Trumpets or Rosh Hashanah was that year. It was to begin in just two days.

Cassi and I spent the morning processing the events of the previous evening. Clearly, we needed to do something to respond to the Lord. One of my questions was, "Can a normal person do a ten-day fast?" The idea of a juice or liquid fast was at the forefront of my mind. I had never done a ten-day fast on only liquids. Neither had Cassi. Here we were, normal people. We resolved to test it out ourselves and see.

While I didn't hear or experience God in special, memorable ways during that time, both Cassi and I look back on that first ten-day fast as a defining moment in our lives. The first step of obedience to the vision was doing it ourselves.

The day after the fast ended, we joined in an incredible city-wide Christian festival. More than a dozen churches and ministries in Santa Fe hosted a unity event on the downtown plaza. Hundreds of people came out to lift the name of Jesus over our city. It seemed to be a small, initial fulfillment of what I had seen in my vision. The city had not stopped but believers from many churches had come together in unity to worship, to pray, and to exalt the name of Jesus over the city. This became the first instance of a pattern that repeated many times in the future: 10 Days partnering with a culminating event in calling the city-wide church together to worship.

AM I GOING CRAZY?

In the aftermath of this powerful encounter and then the season of fasting, normal life set in. And yet, on the inside, nothing was normal for me. I wrestled constantly with how to respond in obedience to the vision.

Obeying the vision was terrifying. Who was I to travel around the country calling people to 10 Days of fasting and repentance? I was most afraid that I would not respond; that I would do nothing and fail to obey what God was calling me to do. That fall, I stepped back from my job as a waiter and took extensive time to write, pray, and plan how to respond to what God had said. I talked about my experience with very few people.

I came from a faith background where hearing from God was not normal or expected, so I lacked a grid for my experiences. While I had good-hearted and wise people in my life, I was afraid to share much with them. I was riddled with doubts, stuck in a loop in my mind. Was this experience from God, or was I going crazy, becoming a religious nut? I needed confirmation from others to know if these seemingly incredible experiences were from God, or if they were just grandiose delusions of my addled brain. One thing was for sure—I didn't want to go tilting at windmills like a second-rate Don Quixote. If this was God, I wanted to pursue it full-heartedly; if it was not I needed to know, and soon.

CONFIRMATION: THE GLOBAL DAY OF PRAYER

Several weeks later, John Robb invited me and about thirty others to come to Albuquerque to hear about a new global prayer initiative. He shared a video telling the story of the Global Day of Prayer, a prayer movement that was emerging from Africa.

The movement, founded by a South African businessman named Graham Power, started in 2001. Led by a word from God, Graham filled a large stadium in Cape Town for a day of prayer and repentance. The event took its main theme from 2 Chronicles 7:14: "If my people who are called by my name will humble themselves, and pray, and seek my face, and turn from their wicked ways, then I will hear from heaven, and I will heal their land."

This Cape Town stadium gathering had overflowed by 2004 into tens of millions joining in stadium gatherings of prayer and repentance throughout every nation of Africa.

The movement was about to go global. The vision was to see hundreds of millions of believers from every nation join in the first ever Global Day of Prayer, planned for Pentecost Sunday, 2005.

Even more amazing to my ears, the Global Day of Prayer was also calling for ten days of united, global prayer leading up to Pentecost Sunday.

My heart leapt. I couldn't believe my ears. God had told me specifically just weeks earlier to "Pray for 10 Days leading up to Pentecost this year (2005)." For some reason, He had independently told me to participate in the first ever Global Day of Prayer.

This made a powerful impression on me—it was the most miraculous thing I had personally experienced. I was not crazy—somehow God was telling me the same thing He was telling a South African businessman.

Coming out of that gathering in Albuquerque, I put aside my doubts. I felt up to that point as if I had been paddling a canoe by myself, in a side pond, all alone. Suddenly I was out in the current—God was driving me forward into the roaring stream of a global prayer movement.

FORWARD MOMENTUM

A conviction was growing in me. I needed to obey what I had seen on the night I received the 10 Days vision. God had showed me that spreading 10 Days was as easy as driving around the nation and sharing with people one-by-one. That was my step of obedience. I needed to do what God had formed me to do from my mother's womb—to start calling cities to stop, repent, unite in prayer, and seek God in unprecedented ways.

I had no idea what I was doing and I knew the task before me was impossible. I also knew my God loved to do impossible things. If I would just respond in faith, He would cause cities to stop and bring unprecedented revival.

In the Scriptures, Jesus sent the disciples out two-by-two. I was acutely aware of how afraid I was, and how timid I could be. I needed a traveling partner. So, I reached out to a younger friend of mine named David and asked if he would be willing to travel with me. In a few weeks, David had said "yes," gotten engaged to his girlfriend, quit his job, and moved across the country.

We were ready to take the nation by storm. 10 Days was an impossible vision, it's true. But we were full of faith that God was about to do impossible things throughout the whole earth.

With the benefit of hindsight, it's clear the power of these first experiences overawed me. I was not used to seeing God do miraculous things and so I over-interpreted the few examples I had.

At the time, it was clear to me that these amazing events were signs that cities were about to stop and repent *en masse*. God was going to send sweeping revival to America in 2005, and David and I were His advance team. With so many incredible things happening, we must be on the verge of a new and greater Pentecost and then possibly the Lord's return. What else could these things mean?

I was about to find out.

5

THE REVIVALISTS (2005)

On January 6, 2005—Epiphany on the church calendar—David and I headed north from Santa Fe, plunging into the greatest adventure of our lives.

We had a makeshift plan in mind. Using his mid-sized Chevy (considerably nicer than my 1986 Lincoln Town-Car), we planned to drive around the United States, show up at various influential churches and ministries, and share the vision of cities shutting down for prayer during the Ten Days of Awe. We had drafted documents explaining "A Time to Mourn," our initial name for 10 Days.

Alongside the fall 10 Days, we would also share about the Global Day of Prayer with a special emphasis on inviting people to take part in the 10 Days of Prayer leading up to Pentecost.

We had a few convictions about how we would implement our plan. First, it was very important for us to be "Incarnational." Incarnational is a big, theological word that means "in the body." But what we meant was we would show up places in person without calling ahead. Somehow, this seemed like real, authentic Christian practice. In hindsight, it's amazing we thought to use the car instead of walking everywhere like Jesus did.

Another major piece of our plan was to give the 10 Days vision away—our goal wasn't to build an organization but rather to give 10 Days away as a gift.

Giving the vision away freely not only reflected God's generous heart; it was also a practical strategy. We were just two kids. David was barely twenty and I was only twenty-three. How was God going to stop entire cities for prayer in 2005 if not through the influence of these larger Christian organizations? However, if some of them said yes to our simple plan, we could see the whole nation and whole world reached in much the way God had showed me.

It just so happened that merely five hours north of Santa Fe sat Colorado Springs, the Mecca of evangelical Christianity. We decided to start this journey of faith by casting vision there to some of the largest Christian organizations in the world.

"FOXES HAVE HOLES..."

We arrived in the Springs late at night, knowing no one and having no contacts. As a money-saving measure, we had resolved to either sleep in the car or in host homes. We had both given up our jobs to do this, and while we were trusting God to provide for our travels, we didn't want to accrue unnecessary expenses.

I have never felt so completely alone as I did that night. My sense of alienation—knowing no one in the city, having nowhere to go, and not understanding what we were even doing—sapped my strength. We slept in the car near the highway in freezing temperatures encircled by mountainous piles of snow. In between frozen, fitful moments of sleep, I felt as though all the demons in hell were circling me. I asked the Lord to give me courage, not knowing how I'd be able to go forward. The entire night I was on the verge of driving home and quitting. It was good I had David there—otherwise, I certainly wouldn't have made it through even the first night. The Scripture that says "Foxes have holes, birds of the air have nests, but the Son of Man has nowhere to lay His head" was circling in my mind as well. If Jesus also felt this way on earth, at least we were in good company.

FIGURING IT OUT

As morning dawned, David and I headed into town for coffee. It was a sink-or-swim moment for us—we needed some positive momentum.

A few months earlier, I had heard a man named Dick Eastman speak. I knew he had a new, large ministry facility called the Jericho Center. Mr. Eastman was a praying man who led a ministry called Every Home for Christ, dedicated to sharing the gospel with every household in the world. He seemed like our kind of guy, and I knew he had dedicated prayer rooms at his facility.

We were pleasantly surprised when the staff let us walk in and use the prayer rooms and building unattended. We tried unsuccessfully to get a meeting with some of the leaders of the ministry. This and several other early failures awakened us to a very simple problem with our "incarnational" approach to ministry—most normal people want to schedule meetings, not just have strangers show up on their doorstep. Was this a problem with American church culture that was too professional, too far removed from the simple gospel? Maybe. But, didn't love for the church compel us to change ourselves to reach our brothers? Absolutely. From then on, we would call ahead.

The Jericho Center facility was massive and had everything we needed—internet access, two prayer rooms, a yellow phonebook, and several landlines we could use near the prayer rooms. The landline was extremely helpful as we had limited minutes on our shared cell phone.

With these resources in hand, we began scouring the phone book and making cold calls. World Prayer Center—sounds promising! Focus on the Family—call them! Compassion International—I've got a kid on my fridge at home, call them! ACSI—who on earth is that? They accredit all the Christian Schools in America? Call them! Big churches, small churches, Young Life, and on and on we went. Colorado Springs was a target-rich environment if your goal is stalking prominent Evangelical ministries.

After a day in the Springs, two things were becoming clear. We were starting to make progress scheduling meetings for the next week. Also, we had no place to sleep that night. With encouragement from a friend, we headed back to Santa Fe, knowing we had "scouted out the land." Our schedule for the following week was already starting to fill up with recognizable names from American Christianity. What would the next week hold?

A SUCCESSFUL WEEK AND SHOCKING NEWS

Back in the comfort of home, we eagerly shared war stories with Cassi. We had made it through the first horrible night. We had a sense of how the city was laid out and knew how to find our way around town. After a handful of in-person meetings, we were gaining confidence. Also, we had a base of operations at the Jericho Center.

The next week, we left at 4 a.m. Monday so we could arrive at the start of business hours, landing at a coffee shop to use the internet and plan the week. We sent a few emails, made a few calls, and before long, our week began to fill up with meetings.

Colorado Springs was in the midst of a January warm snap. With warm sunshine and unseasonable temperatures in the mid-60's, it was the exact opposite of the previous week. As the temperature warmed, we were starting to heat up as well. That week, we had two to five meetings scheduled each day. We were starting to get the hang of this.

We met with the prayer director of Compassion International. She was an older woman who was kind, warm, and receptive to our naivete and simple faith. She lovingly told us that she would share the vision for the Global Day of Prayer and the 10 Days leading up to Pentecost with her entire network. Was our wild plan actually starting to work?

We met with two gentlemen at Focus on the Family. Focus, more than any other ministry, seemed like a juggernaut of American Christianity. If somehow they would say "yes" to 10 Days, surely cities would soon be shutting down. As we spoke, the two men dashed our hopes; they were simply middle management, cogs in a larger machine, and didn't have the power to get Focus to adopt 10 Days of fasting and mourning. As they explained, Focus was an "aircraft carrier" and it didn't turn on a dime. The men were middle-aged and clearly a bit jaded by corporate Christian culture. They also found us to be slightly obnoxious—clearly, this was not their normal Tuesday afternoon meeting. Tempted as we were by this encounter to look down on Focus and "corporate Christianity," we fought against it, blessed them, and began praying that these large, "aircraft carrier" ministries would learn how to surf, being led by the wind and waves of the Holy Spirit. We were navigating rejection, turning it into prayer, and coming out loving our brothers on the other side.

One of the highlights of the week was a meeting at the World Prayer Center at New Life Church, the biggest church in the Springs. As we entered the main prayer room, a cavernous space with an enormous, free-standing globe at the front, live worship and prayer was happening in the middle of the workday. I could sense God's presence as I walked into the room. A handful of people were praying and worshiping in this large room. To my left, I saw a middle-aged woman. As I saw her worshiping no-holds-barred, I could "see" from God that this woman was incredibly beautiful to Him. With an uncharacteristic boldness, I walked up to her.

"God says that you are beautiful to Him," I said, part of me thinking "This must be the most awkward thing anyone has ever said."

And yet, she thanked me and broke down sobbing, touched by the power of God. This was one of my first times having this type of experience, delivering a prophetic message to someone personally, although I wouldn't have used that language at the time.

The director of the World Prayer Center welcomed us into his office. He was receptive to the vision we shared, especially the Global Day of Prayer. However, the highlight of our meeting was when he began speaking prophetically over David. He knew specific details about David's life and spoke about how God was laying claim to David's heart. The word left David shaken.

STEPPING INTO THE BIBLE

For David and me, young men with spiritual hunger but very limited experience of God's supernatural power, it was as though we had stepped into the pages of the Bible. Amazing God encounters were happening all around us, through us, and to us. We were constantly in a state of awe. It seemed we witnessed more miraculous events in that first week than in our entire lives up to that point.

Not only that, but we experienced close fellowship as we pursued this mission together, sharing both our trials and possessions in common, praying together constantly, and doing our best to obey Jesus's command to "love one another as I have loved you." Like David and Jonathan in the Bible, we really loved each other.

Worn down by sleeping in the car, we went to a local Presbyterian church looking for someone to show us hospitality. David, more shameless and bold as a rule, walked right into their elders meeting and asked if someone would take us in. And one of the elders agreed. The exchange was awkward but if it meant not sleeping in the car, it was worth it. And even if it was weird, it was biblical. The Bible says elders should show hospitality to traveling believers.

As we drove back to Santa Fe at the end of the week, we were riding high. We had met leaders from more than a dozen ministries, seen God speak and move powerfully, and frankly, we were full of God. Working for God was liberating, amazing, supernatural. Had this been the most amazing week of my life?

At that point of exultation and praise to God, our cell phone rang.

It was my wife Cassi.

"I'm pregnant," she said.

"Oh s***," I said, not the best reaction of all time for a father-to-be.

I was in shock.

"This is the worst possible time for this to happen," I thought to myself, even as I tried to encourage Cassi.

We had just launched out on an impossible mission to call the nation into ten days of prayer, repentance, and mourning. My faith was stretched to the limit. How could God give us a new child on top of it all? And yet, by the time we finished the drive back to Santa Fe, I had come to my senses. This was the best news I had ever received. I was going to be a father. This really was the most amazing week of my life!

PRAYING THROUGH

After a weekend of celebration in Santa Fe, David and I headed back to the Springs.

We had found our rhythm. While no one had committed their organization to doing the fall 10 Days, we had several positive commitments from major Christian organizations to the Global Day of Prayer. Also, we were seeing God move supernaturally every day. We were "on fire" as never before, trusting in God and walking in His presence on a moment-by-moment basis.

Working for God was the most incredible thing I had ever done.

During a midweek prayer service, I received a call from Cassi. She was bleeding and worried she was losing the baby. As I stepped outside the church, it felt like a knife had been twisted in my stomach. I fell to my knees in pain and prayer. For the first time in my life, I had some inkling of what it meant to be a father.

I prayed with Cassi outside the church until the bleeding stopped. At the time, I was reading E.M. Bounds, a well-known teacher on prayer. Bounds would talk about "praying through" situations until a conviction of faith came. I wasn't sure I had ever experienced that before, but I saw Bounds as a reliable guide.

That night, Cassi called again at about two a.m. The bleeding had returned. While I started out feeling exhausted and discouraged, as we prayed on the phone, I sensed faith rise up in me for this child to live. It's hard to explain, but after about forty-five minutes of prayer, a change occurred, as though everything came into order and was clear. "This must be what Bounds described as 'praying through'," I thought. Doubt was replaced with complete confidence that God had heard my prayer—the child would surely live.

As we began to drive back to Santa Fe, I experienced another first in prayer, something I would describe as a "spirit of might." It was as though the power of God entered the vehicle as I prayed for my baby. It was an intense experience of spiritual warfare. While experiencing this unusual grace, it seemed to me I was powerfully warring not only for the child's life and destiny, not only for my wife, but also for the entire nation to be awakened and for the veil of spiritual darkness to be broken off the church. The presence of God was so strong in the car that David didn't know what to make of it. He became visibly afraid and started repenting.

While the drive started on a high note, I was exhausted and deflated by the time we arrived home. My earlier faith for the baby to live and powerful experiences in prayer now seemed like a distant memory. I did my best to comfort Cassi, but I was profoundly unsettled. The next day, we went to the hospital for an ultrasound. The baby was gone.

I could not believe it. I knew God had heard my prayers—was this just to test my faith? Being dead was not a problem for God. Over the past few days I had experienced so many breakthroughs in prayer, sensed God's power and presence as never before, and known that I was praying in faith and would receive what I was asking.

The answer, I felt, was to push myself harder, to become more intense, and to pray MORE. I would stay up all night, praying all night for the baby to be raised. Certainly, then the child would come back to life.

I did my best to spend the entire night on my knees, pleading with God, and yet to no avail. For some reason, pushing myself into greater and greater intensity of prayer, of perseverance, of "faith" wasn't working.

A CRISIS OF FAITH

Up to that point, I had never been one to blame God for bad things in life. Many of the bad things that happened were clearly the result of my own bad decisions or character flaws. Other times, bad things simply happened in a fallen world. I was not naïve about evil. I knew that God had promised we would endure troubles and difficulties in this life; I expected them and thought I was ready for them.

However, just two weeks into my journey to call the world to 10 Days of mourning, fasting, and repentance, I had discovered something that I was not prepared to face.

Just saying "yes" to this calling had required all the courage I could muster. When I found out Cassi was expecting, it was a shock, but I had risen to the occasion. When she started bleeding, I had "prayed through" to the place of faith. I had experienced the power of God in prayer unlike anything I had ever experienced before. I was doing my best and giving everything I had to the Lord. How could God ask so much from me and then allow this to happen? How could He give me these powerful experiences in prayer, leading me to believe He was hearing me and then let our baby die?

This felt like a personal betrayal, like God Himself had set me up. I found myself seriously struggling, not only with mourning the loss of our child, but with the goodness of God. Was this the kind of God that I want to serve?

The only thing that did make sense was this: God had told me to call His people to mourning. And now, I was in mourning unlike anything else I had ever experienced, mourning for our only child. Both Cassi and I had long hair at the time. Both of us shaved our heads.

I spoke to my aunt about it, who was my personal pastor and a wise voice of counsel. I laid out my case against God in painstaking detail. She listened, and wisely admonished me that while it truly didn't make sense, God's character hadn't changed because of what I had gone through. Not understanding what was happening was not a reason to blame God's character. Like a cruel knife, this loss had pierced my armor and cut to the very core of who I was. I didn't know what to do, and I didn't understand.

Although David and I attempted to keep traveling immediately after this, it was pointless. I didn't have the strength to talk to anyone and would just sit alone in the car, crying. David, now my caretaker, wisely took us drove us back to Santa Fe. We were forced to take about ten days off to mourn.

CITY OF ANGELS

After more than a week of mourning, I didn't understand what had happened any better. Nothing about it made sense. However, I had recovered enough that I could talk to people without bursting into tears. I knew it was time to get back to work. David and I drove out to Los Angeles where we spent most of the month of February.

At first, I hated LA. The superficiality, the pace, the smog, the traffic. If any place was Babylon, this had to be it. Our first visit was to a large, well-known church. The place was massive, a strange hybrid of a church, a mall, and Disneyland. We tried to have a generous attitude, but it was far removed from the expression of Christianity we were longing to see. And yet, as we started making phone calls, we began to have one amazing meeting after another. Against all odds, I was falling in love with LA.

A young film writer from a hip, young-adult church took us into his apartment near Hollywood. We slept in his living room and stayed up late talking about the Lord and the intersection of faith and art. We met Charles Kraft, a professor at Fuller Seminary and expert on deliverance ministry. We had meetings with the leaders at famous ministries, like the US Center for World Missions, the Trinity Broadcasting Network, Faithful Central Bible Church, Saddleback Church, and many others.

One day we attended a meeting at Hollywood Presbyterian Church. After sharing about 10 Days, the pastor gave us the name and phone number of a key city-wide prayer leader and suggested that we get in touch with him.

As David and I walked back to our car, I tried to call the prayer leader, but got a voice mail.

As I put the phone back in my pocket, I heard the Holy Spirit say, "The man you're looking for is here."

David was well ahead of me, calling for me to catch up so we could get to our next meeting. We were already running late. Just as I was about to ignore the voice and go with David, I turned and walked back the way we had come.

"It doesn't make sense for him to be here, but this man must be here." I thought to myself.

David, exasperated, threw his arms up, and came back to drag me to our next meeting by force if necessary. Just then, two men and a woman walked up a set of stairs and emerged into the courtyard.

"One of these men must be the city-wide prayer leader," I thought. The three of them were lost in conversation but thankfully, they were wearing nametags. Sure enough, it was him. Holy Spirit had led me right to the key prayer leader for Hollywood, California.

As we drove throughout Southern California, David and I made a point of praying big prayers and turning our car into a prayer room. When we arrived in LA, the first thing we noticed was the smog, clinging to the horizon like a ring of scum on a toilet. We saw this as a natural image of the spiritual darkness over the region. So, we asked God to remove it. As had happened in Colorado Springs, the weather in LA was unusual. Although the region is known for drought, as we started getting breakthroughs in our meetings, it started raining and it didn't stop until the day before we left. As we left LA after three weeks, we looked in our rear-view mirror and saw the unbelievable: the rain had washed the smog away. God had heard our prayers.

TAKING ON THE NATION

After LA, we settled into a pattern. We'd return to Santa Fe every week or two. We would arrive in a new town—Phoenix, St. Louis, Chicago, Kansas City, and many others, set up three to five meetings a day, share the vision, and then move on. We continued having divine appointments, hearing God's voice, and seeing answers to prayer.

However, most often when we shared about 10 Days, we experienced confusion and indifference from our hearers. Sharing the vision was hard for me: it felt like pulling my heart out of my chest and putting it on the table several times a day to complete strangers. Most often, the offering was not understood or received. The pain of being rejected by hundreds of people was beginning to pile up.

I had told the Lord no one would want to stop and pray for ten days, but I didn't realize it would be this bad. While a few people had decided to join in the Global Day of Prayer, almost no one was resonating with the vision of stopping everything for mourning during the Ten Days of Awe. 10 Days was a gift we were giving away—the problem was, it was a gift no one wanted.

We continued to sleep a little, travel a lot, and generally push the limits of what our bodies could handle. As young men, we hadn't quite figured out if there was a limit to how little sleep we needed, to how far we could travel, and how much we could do for the Lord in a day, but we thought we would find out. And whenever we were tired, my solution was always to push harder, sleep less, and do more. The Lord had given me an important assignment, and I didn't want to fail Him.

CRACKS BEGIN TO SHOW

By late March, I was exhibiting erratic behavior.

While traveling in St. Louis, I became angry at a well-known ministry I believed was preaching a false gospel. The obvious solution, or so it seemed to me, was for us to walk into their main building, stand up on a table, and publicly call them to repentance for their sins. David pleaded with me and even physically restrained me from marching into their ministry headquarters and denouncing them.

"Maybe you don't have what it takes to do what God has called us to do," I said bitterly, as David kept me from making one of the biggest mistakes of my life. I was furious at him for standing in my way.

A PERFECT STORM

As we moved toward the first 10 Days, a perfect storm of circumstances was beginning to swirl. Rather than slow down, my answer was always to push harder. More prayer. More urgency. More intensity. More force. I didn't want to let God down. We had to give it everything we had.

And yet, we were running out of money. I had started the trip with about $7,000 in savings and we were "living by faith," trusting God to provide for our finances. The problem was that money was almost used up and nothing new was coming our way.

David and I routinely functioned on two to four hours of sleep each night, often sleeping in our car. The lifestyle of 24/7 travel was starting to take a toll.

Cassi was unhappy and struggling because of my long absences. She bought a puppy to keep her company while I was away, but my style of ministry was beginning to severely tax our marriage.

I was still struggling with feelings that God had betrayed me and feared He would do it again. I knew this was wrong and I tried to shove those feelings down, but they always seemed to pop up when they were least helpful.

Although we were sharing the vision three to five times a day, only a handful of people had committed to 10 Days leading up to Pentecost and no one had committed to the Ten Days of Awe. Our long journey was starting to look like a failure. What were we doing wrong?

I didn't know why, but my personality was changing. I was now prone to doing and saying rash, uncharacteristic things. I was becoming judgmental, angry, and unstable. Like Elijah in the Old Testament, I felt I was the last man in the entire nation who was following God.

Washington, D.C. was the last place we cast vision before Pentecost. We visited a ministry that had been recommended as "the best group of praying young people" in the USA. And yet, many of the people we connected with seemed shallow and erratic, even by our standards. Could this really be the best group of praying young people in our nation?

More appealing to me was the life of a local friend who let us stay in his apartment. He had an office job in a government agency and took us out with his sophisticated, professional friends. It felt strange, like I was a disheveled, John the Baptist figure who had to go out in polite society to a fancy restaurant. The appeal of an urbane life with a good paycheck and smart friends was a powerful reminder of what I had sacrificed to follow Jesus. Now, a year later, I was starting to wonder if I had made the right choice.

With these winds swirling around us, we entered the build up to our first 10 Days event. David and I decided that in the weeks leading up to the 10 Days and the Global Day of Prayer, we would stop traveling and help organize a 10 Days of Prayer expression in St. Louis, our hometown. God had told me "You are going to pray for 10 Days leading up to Pentecost this year," so I knew it was important.

I could tell I was almost completely poured out. Even though I had given so much, it seemed like nothing was happening. I held out hope that the God of the impossible would break in just at the last possible moment. I was willing to give everything to follow Him; now He just needed to do His part, pour out His Spirit, and bring the vision of cities stopping and sweeping revival to pass.

6

THE FIRST 10 DAYS (2005)

THE first 10 Days in 2005 is one of the most encouraging testimonies I have in my repertoire.

I strongly suspect it is not possible for anyone to do 10 Days worse than we did that year. So take heart, whatever you're doing wrong, it's not as bad as what we did in 2005.

David and I landed in St. Louis to begin planning the first 10 Days. The Global Day of Prayer team in the city welcomed us with open arms. They were happy to have a group focused on the 10 Days leading up to Pentecost, while they focused on the Global Day of Prayer event scheduled at Busch Stadium, home of the St. Louis Cardinals.

Our expectations as a team for massive, immanent revival were sky-high. And yet, in all my experience, I can't think of a team I've been a part of that has been more consistently discouraged or faced more obstacles and failure. Somehow, nothing we did seemed to work.

EMPTY THE TANK

At that point, I had a one-year vision for 10 Days and expected everything I had seen in the vision to happen that year. The fact that it looked impossible was not a problem. It was supposed to look impossible. That was the point. I just needed to have faith. God was going to come through. He had to come through.

My plan was simple. I was going to give God everything I had left. I would empty myself and leave it all on the altar. I thought if I could only lay my life down completely, God would respond, cities would stop, and incredible revival would break out.

I was already so worn down I was barely functional. I tried my old trick of working through the phonebook, calling all the churches in St. Louis. This time I was too depressed to make more than one or two calls. The constant vulnerability to strangers, the rejection, the daily routine of being misunderstood had created a wound I didn't yet understand.

My erratic behavior was getting worse. Friends who had not seen me in the past year could see something was off. I knew something was wrong, but I couldn't put my finger on it. My mood was swinging wildly, either high on expectation for revival or down and depressed, unable to carry on a normal conversation. But now, it was becoming harder and harder to find those highs. The patience and love for others I started with had eroded. I was harsh, judgmental, and had an apocalyptic mindset. Was I becoming one of those guys holding a sign, "The end is near?" Was I becoming a religious fanatic?

We printed and distributed thousands of flyers on bulletin boards throughout the city, inviting people to the 10 Days of Prayer. While I was too weak to do cold-calling, Cassi stepped up and called hundreds of congregations in the city, inviting the whole world to join 10 Days and the Global Day of Prayer. We might be crash-landing into this first 10 Days, but we were going to make it.

WATCH THE CARDINALS

It is remarkable how in the darkest times, when everything seems to be falling apart, God so often sends encouragement in unexpected ways.

While I had my own struggles, the entire Global Day of Prayer team in St. Louis was incredibly discouraged. It seemed like everything that could go wrong was going wrong. One of our leaders was a pastor named Vic Gerson. Vic was in his forties and had a famous brother, Michael Gerson, President Bush's speechwriter at the time.

Right in the middle of our corporate discouragement, Vic threw his back out while working on a flooring project. Injury had been added to insult. Lying on his back, unable to even move, he began to complain to God about how poorly our efforts were going.

The Lord spoke an unlikely phrase to him: "Watch the Cardinals." Vic was not a baseball fan and didn't watch games regularly. However, he did pay attention to the next game, which was being played on Monday, May second, just before the beginning of 10 Days that Thursday.

That night, the Cardinals came into the ninth inning trailing 9-3. After two outs, the score was 9-4. But then, amazingly, the Cardinals came back to win the game 10-9. It was the largest ninth inning comeback in team history.

I was a little offended to be honest—can God speak through baseball games? Is that allowed? And yet, that was one of the most miraculous things I had ever witnessed first-hand.

The lesson of Vic's "Watch the Cardinals" word seemed pretty simple. Though it looked like we were losing badly—and we all felt that way—God was saying that He had a ninth inning miracle rally that would pull us out of defeat and cause us to win, "10 to 9."

I felt like this must mean that even though it looked bleak now, the outpouring of the Spirit I was seeking would come in just a few days on the first ever Global Day of Prayer.

At the time, I didn't pause to consider if I was misinterpreting this remarkable sign. Could it be that the game was just beginning, and God was saying, "it may look like you're losing for a long time but don't give up?" The thought never entered my mind. I was single-mindedly focused on pushing myself across the finish line of Pentecost Sunday, May 15, 2005.

10 DAYS

David and I had a plan—not a good plan, but a plan—to gather an entire city together in prayer. We decided to have three locations throughout the city that would be open for prayer 24/7. We had cold-called hundreds of churches, put up thousands of flyers, gone on the radio, and shared at schools and public settings, inviting anyone who would listen to join us.

But there was a major problem with our plan. Almost no one wanted to pray.

Because we had three locations (due to expecting the entire city to stop and join us), our small, committed team of five people needed to split up. David based his small prayer group at a Roman Catholic church that opened their doors for prayer. Cassi and I ended up at an inner-city mission on Grand Avenue in North St. Louis. Our new prayer room was in one of the most depressed and crime-ridden areas in the entire nation. With bombed out houses littering the cityscape, open prostitution and drug dealing on the street, and a murder rate that would make Detroit blush, we were in a hard part of town.

My dad had wisely informed me that people would not want to come there to pray. It was dangerous. However, in my religious zeal,

I was incapable of reasoning like a normal human being. All I could think was that the heart of darkness was the perfect place to pray. If people didn't want to go there, it reflected how far away they were from God's heart.

As we started the 10 Days, modeling our prayer room on the 24/7 movement I had read about in Red Moon Rising, I learned something I hadn't really known before. It is incredibly difficult to do 24/7 prayer. And, in case you are wondering, two people are not enough to sustain 24/7 prayer.

Since almost no one had responded to our attempts to unite the city, Cassi and I were attempting to pray the entire time on our own. It was like trying to bail out the Titanic with a bucket. Rather than settle on a smaller, simpler schedule that we could effectively keep, we tried to do 24/7 prayer and ended up being totally sporadic. It was mostly the two of us in a room together. We slept, ate, and attempted to pray at the base—an old, converted YMCA. Once again, I was pushing us beyond our physical capabilities. It would have been quite funny if it hadn't been so sad.

In this state of despondency, the Lord was faithful to speak to us. I heard Him speak out of Revelation 2:10:

"Do not fear what you are about to suffer. Behold, the devil is about to cast some of you into prison so that you will be tested and you will have tribulation for ten days. Be faithful unto death and I will give you the crown of life."

While this wasn't the most encouraging word I have ever heard, it was accurate. The cinder-block mission we were living in felt like a prison. When we walked outside, we were surrounded by blighted homes and inner-city neighbors who viewed us with suspicion. I wasn't even sure if it was God talking, but 10 Days of tribulation and testing seemed to be happening.

NO ONE COMES

By far, the biggest source of discouragement was the near-complete rejection from other believers of what I was sharing. Since January sixth, I had cast vision to hundreds of ministry leaders in person. We had invited and spoken personally to thousands of people in St. Louis. I was so discouraged that almost no one had responded to the invitation.

The ministry that graciously hosted 10 Days of Prayer was also not interested in praying. In total, they prayed only one hour out of the 240. When they came into prayer for that one hour, while Cassi and I were gone, a man walked into the prayer room off the street and ask how to be saved. It seemed so easy—if we prayed, God would move and hear us. And yet no one wanted to stop what they were doing to pray.

Rather than patiently enduring, understanding, and forgiving my brothers and sisters, the lack of response began to cut a deep resentment in my heart.

On the seventh day, Cassi and I were finally able to step away from the mission for lunch. It was our first time leaving the building since 10 Days had started. Getting out of the prayer room and north St. Louis was like taking a breath after a long dive underwater. I felt hope rising up in my chest.

However, when we arrived back at the mission, our four-month-old puppy, Sequoia, jumped out the open car door and rushed into traffic. A sweet older woman who lived up the side-street was driving past at just that moment and hit her. Cassi and I rushed Sequoia to the vet, and amazingly, she lived. However, she never regained the function of her front left leg.

I had imagined praying for ten days would be challenging but rewarding. This was shaping up to be the worst ten days of my life.

A NEW PENTECOST?

As the 10 Days began to wind down, I could tell I was almost spent, yet I wanted to finish strong. The Saturday night before Pentecost, we hosted a late-night Scripture reading vigil, focused on the book of Psalms. Several others joined us and we were able to cover most of the night as we read the entire book of Psalms out loud. It was a powerful time of prayer and the closest we came to sustaining even a single day of 24/7 prayer.

As Pentecost approached, despite my extreme weariness and just wanting to quit and be done, I still anticipated God coming through in a massive way. I was looking for a Pentecostal outpouring on Pentecost. After all, I had done what God said. David and I had been obedient; we had traveled the country inviting people to stop everything and seek God's face. We had done our part, or so we hoped, and now it was time for God to do what only He could do. Even though everything felt horrible and unattainable, it would all be worth it when God came through with an impossible, last-minute victory.

As we attended Memorial Presbyterian Church on Pentecost Sunday, May 15, I was crying out, "God, send a new Pentecost." At times, it felt so close. And yet, the reality was while it was a good church service, it was far from Acts chapters 1 and 2.

"Did I just lay down my entire life for a good church service?" I wondered.

And I felt, with some justification, that I really had laid down my life.

Since receiving the 10 Days vision, I had quit my paying job and given all my time and energy to traveling the nation and calling people to pray. I had lost my first child to miscarriage. My dog had lost a leg. My wife had been in crisis multiple times because of my extended absences and our marriage was rocky.

I had also lost heroes and friends. My closest relationships were strained to the breaking point. I had spent my life savings. I had laid my heart on the table day after day, to the point that now my soul was in agony from the pain of so much vulnerability, so much rejection. I had given so much to the church while getting nothing but pain in return. I was at the breaking point.

That afternoon, I attended the Global Day of Prayer gathering at Busch Stadium. We had hoped to fill Busch Stadium, but only 3,000 people came. While 3,000 people is certainly a large prayer meeting, in a stadium designed for over 40,000, it looked like a drop in the bucket. As I sat there, it suddenly dawned on me—there was not going to be an outpouring. This was it. A bad prayer meeting with 3,000 people. This is what I had given everything in my life for.

Several things were perfectly clear to me.

One was that I had totally wasted my life and wasted my time.

Second, I had given absolutely everything for the church, my fellow believers. While I had laid down everything, they wouldn't even turn off the TV on a Sunday afternoon and come to one measly prayer meeting. I had given my all for them, but they had not responded. And I hated them. I really, really hated Christians.

Finally, I had mixed feelings about God. Part of me wanted to accuse Him of letting me down. However, mostly I just felt like a failure. He had shown me this amazing vision; I had done everything I knew how to bring it to pass; but I had failed. I had given everything I had, everything I could possibly think of giving, but it had not been enough. I had laid my life down as best I could but the miracle hadn't happened.

Heartbroken, and in utter agony, I told the Lord, "God, you are too intense for me. I quit."

Thus ended my first ever 10 Days of Prayer.

7

THE CRASH (2005-2006)

AFTER five months on the road, casting vision for 10 Days hundreds of times, meeting thousands of people, and seeing God move as never before in my life, I had completely crashed.

Just nine months after an incredible visionary experience had transformed my life, I handed in my resignation papers. In less than a year, I had gone from quitting my job for God to quitting my job with God. I had gone from "on fire" to flameout.

I was not the only one who was crashing.

The circle of believing friends from St. Louis that David and I were a part of fell apart. Everyone in our tight-knit community went their own way, with lots of hard feelings, blame casting, and resentments.

A few weeks after the first 10 Days, David returned to Santa Fe one last time to pick up his things. It became clear to me then how deeply he was hurt. He blamed me for the problems we had encountered and the pain he was experiencing.

David deeply hated me. In the span of weeks, we had gone from closest friends to worst enemies. David's crash was even worse than mine. Within a few months, he had left his fiancé—a godly woman—and then completely left the faith, full of rage against God and me.

To be honest, I wanted to join David and completely walk away from God. Before having significant encounters with the Lord in 2003, I had struggled with frequent depression. Walking closely with the Holy Spirit had changed everything and chased my depression away. Now, it was back and worse than it had ever been.

"This must be demonic," I thought.

My mind was filled continually with hatred, accusation, and negative thoughts, directed at myself and at others. For some reason, I could not remember any of the good or miraculous things God had done in my life. I had no idea how to escape this mental prison. I thought about King Saul in the Bible, who disobeyed God, lost his calling, and then was tormented by evil spirits in his mind.

"I must be a Saul," I reasoned.

I had blown my chance, and God had utterly cast me off. Although I wanted to walk away from the Lord completely, somehow, I resisted this temptation. How? I harnessed the one thing I had in abundance—self-hatred—and used it to yoke myself to the Lord.

I reasoned like this:

"Past Me was clearly naïve, a little bit crazy, ignorant, and stupid. However, Past Me was a much better person than Present Me. I may have been off in the past, but however wrong I was then, it was more right than I am right now. Present Me is not a person I should trust."

I resolved not to make any major decisions, like leaving my faith, until my mental state was better.

Many factors had contributed to burnout. Running out of money was a major pain point. When I quit my job to travel the nation and share about 10 Days, I was inspired by George Mueller, the orphanage builder from England who never asked people for finances. He simply prayed and asked God to provide the funds that he needed. Using this unconventional fundraising strategy, he saw miraculous provision totaling millions of dollars throughout his life. I believed that God would do the same thing for me that He did for Mueller.

I had completely thrown myself into this new calling, quitting my paying job and spending all our finances. God had not come through as I expected, and we had run out of money. I felt like a fool. A few weeks after the Global Day of Prayer, I was back working overtime at my old job as a waiter in Santa Fe.

"If God can't be trusted, I might as well take care of myself and make as much money as I can," I reasoned.

Work was the best thing to distract my mind from self-hatred, bitterness, and despair. My prayer life, which had been my fortress, no longer existed. I couldn't connect with God at all.

I was angry with Him: I had given my all and He had completely let me down. Paradoxically, I also felt like the failure was completely my fault. God had given me this beautiful vision to see cities stop everything to pray and repent. I had tried to bring it to pass, but I had failed.

I considered the possibility that I was a false prophet, someone actually working against God. And yet, the signs we had seen along the way, the incredible gift of God's presence we often experienced, and the love we had for other believers at different points in the journey seemed to testify that I wasn't a false prophet—at least not entirely.

In the midst of this breakdown, Cassi was incredible. I was more of a child than a husband. As close relationships all around me crumbled, I wondered if we would make it.

"Are we getting divorced?" I asked her.

"As far as I'm concerned, we are going to stick together no matter what," she responded.

DEPRESSED ENOUGH TO GO TO SEMINARY

In the depths of this burnout experience, Cassi and I flew to Boston for a friend's wedding. The day of our flight, I was in full melt-down mode. I was barely able to function normally at the airport.

Once we arrived in Massachusetts, I felt a little more hopeful. Summer on the New England seacoast was charming: vibrant green and beautiful in an entirely different way from the beloved mountains of the desert southwest. While there, we visited Gordon-Conwell Seminary for the first time. I had applied the previous year but had delayed admission due to my travels. The northeast appealed to us as one of the few areas of the country neither of us had ever lived. It seemed like a nice place to spend a few years, but we knew we would never want to live there permanently. It seemed like a good place to go to school.

When we returned to Santa Fe, the depression kicked into high gear. Trying to cope and trying to pray, I took one of my patented late-night walks. For reasons unknown to me, everyone in Santa Fe seemed to be sitting out on their front porches. I soon realized it was the Fourth of July and fireworks were being staged on a series of trails near our home. I ended up blundering unexpectedly within yards of the professionals setting off a massive, city-wide fireworks display. The workers frantically waved for me to get out of the way as fiery debris rained around my head, missing me by inches. I ducked and covered as flames rained down, running as fast as I could to get out of the hellish barrage.

On that fiery walk, I came to a decision. There was nothing else for us in Santa Fe. I was badly depressed and at the very least we needed to try something different.

"I'm so depressed I guess I'll go to seminary," I said to myself.

SPIRITUAL SIBERIA

We packed all our earthly goods, along with a sack of New Mexico Green Chile and our wounded and now especially beloved dog, Sequoia, and headed for Massachusetts. Somehow, everything managed to fit into our 1986 Lincoln Towncar.

We arranged a winter rental on a beautiful barrier island north of Boston: Plum Island in Newburyport, Massachusetts. Our backyard was a sandy beach that led to a tidal basin where the Merrimac River met the Atlantic Ocean. This lovely setting, lightly populated in the fall and winter months, seemed like the mercy of God. Cassi was pregnant for a second time, another kindness.

In spite of these mercies, I struggled to see God at work. The way I saw it, I had failed Him. I was a bad boy, and He was punishing me by sending me to the least Christian part of the country. I had been sentenced to spiritual Siberia in the frozen Northeast!

My first attempts at being a seminary student were rocky. I was barely hanging on as a believer. Mentally and emotionally, I was barely functioning. At registration, I burst into tears and Cassi had to almost lead me by the hand. I dropped out of several classes in frustration because I couldn't handle the workload. For the first time in my life, I was not a good student. Like Sequoia, who hopped along on only three working legs, I was walking with a limp.

Hoping to regain any sense of connection to God, I had signed up for a class I thought might help. It was called "Personal Evangelism" and taught by Dr. Sam Schutz, a kindly older professor. He was also a practicing psychologist with open office hours. I booked a thirty-minute session with him.

As I began telling Dr. Schutz about my five months traveling the country, I promptly broke down in tears for the entire session. When my thirty minutes were up, he handed me a tissue, and gently but firmly informed me it was time to go. He suggested I reach out to a friend of his named Fred Vyn. Fred had regular sessions of inner healing prayer at a nearby Episcopal Church. I booked a time with Fred's group on October thirty-first.

A GAZELLE SIGHTING

While I certainly believed in the Holy Spirit and had quite a few experiences with Him, I remained quite skeptical of most Charismatic Christians. Coming from my conservative, evangelical church background, I was concerned some of them dipped into "New Age" philosophy. I was open to miraculous things happening as they did in the Bible, but I was also cautious and worried about demonic influence. While I was desperate for help and thankful for the opportunity to receive ministry, in the back of my mind a voice was saying "Watch out for the New Age stuff."

As the time of healing prayer began, I was impressed with how the two prayer ministers, Fred and a woman, seemed to be really listening, both to God and to me. The expressions on their faces seemed to radiate love and compassion.

I shared my journey: I had given everything to obey the vision God had given me, tried to get the entire United States to stop everything for 10 Days of Prayer, believed God would respond with sweeping revival, and had somehow fallen flat on my face.

Fred, with a smile and a chuckle, commented, "We've never had a situation quite like this before."

I had to laugh too. It was a strange story.

As the two of them ministered, Fred commended me for my soldierly obedience.

"You clearly understand God as your Captain, your Commander, your Lord. You're willing to follow Him anywhere and give up anything. In fact, you probably could teach me a thing or two about that," he said.

"Yes, yes," I thought. "That's right; I understand God that way." It was nice to be understood and even get a compliment.

"However, have you ever met Jesus…" he paused for effect, "…as a gazelle?"

"Oh no, here it is," I thought. "I knew they would bring in this New Age garbage!"

However, my mild, mid-western manners led me to respond, "I'm sorry, I don't really know what you mean."

"I mean, have you ever met Jesus as He is presented in the Song of Songs?"

Suddenly, I was aware of just how badly I had misjudged the situation. I was accusing this man in my heart of being "New Age." The only thing he was guilty of was knowing his Bible better than me.

The Song of Songs was a part of the Bible that never made much sense to me. I knew the love affair in the book was often interpreted as a symbolical picture of the love of Christ and the church. But personally, I had never understood or enjoyed the book.

"No, I haven't," I managed to reply. It was true. I had never met Jesus as a gazelle.

As the session continued, Fred and the team "read my mail"—hearing accurately from God and telling me things only God and I knew. They identified how hurtful words and wounds from believers I met on the trip played a key role in my current state and helped me identify specific moments where I had been deeply hurt. They helped me forgive individuals who had wronged me.

WISE COUNSEL

Along with insight into my need to know Jesus as He is described in the Song of Songs, Fred was full of wisdom in other areas.

His counsel helped me understand my one-year timetable for the fulfillment of the 10 Days vision was completely wrong and had set me up for failure. This was a longer-term call from God.

He also reframed events in a very helpful way.

"Last time you tried to get the whole nation to participate. That's not how things usually work. Usually, big things start off small. Why don't you first try to do it yourself, in a small way?" he asked.

Fred put his finger on another glaring problem. I was a hard worker who did not know how to rest. He showed me from the Scriptures how Sabbath rest was key to entering the promises of God. My propensity to work harder and harder for God was unbelief masquerading as religious duty.

Having pushed myself beyond the breaking point, I now felt guilty for not being able to work hard.

Fred asked me a simple question, "What do you enjoy doing right now?"

"The only things I really enjoy right now are cooking and watching movies with my wife."

"Well, do more of that," he said sagely.

The team ended our time together, recognizing there was more healing needed, but also that we had done as much as possible for one night. I left our session a changed man. I was still a mess, but my trajectory had completely changed. I was now firmly headed toward healing and wholeness.

For the first time, I was beginning to understand what had happened to me and why I had crashed and burned.

WISDOM TO WALK IN REVIVAL

That night launched me into a season of personal study and growth that would last several years. I began to have Biblical language to understand my experience of dynamic personal revival followed by dramatic burnout. As I soon learned, I was far from the first person to have such an experience. When God's Spirit has been poured out throughout history, along with the miracles, salvations, and transformed lives I longed for, there have also been heresies, burnouts, and broken lives. In hindsight, it was only the undeserved mercy of God that kept me from completely shipwrecking my faith.

Like all powerful things, the outpouring of God's Spirit can cause great harm if we respond improperly. Just look at what happened to Ananias and Saphira in the book of Acts. Fred and his team had pointed me in the right direction. Over the next months and years, I would dig into the Scriptures and history of past revivals to understand why I had crashed. I was not only looking for personal wholeness—I wanted to learn how groups of believers and even the entire church could sustain a move of God through a lifetime and even generations.

GETTING WISDOM: THE PROVERBS

One Scripture seemed to perfectly describe what had happened to me.

Proverbs 19:2-3: "It is not good to have zeal without knowledge, nor to be hasty and miss the way. A man's own foolishness subverts his way, but his heart rages against the LORD."

Clearly, I had zeal without knowledge. Hastiness and urgency had defined all my actions. Whenever I faced an obstacle, I had one solution: push harder and add more urgency. Clearly, I had taken a wrong turn and missed the way. My own foolishness had led to a train wreck and my heart was raging against God. I was a living, breathing embodiment of this Proverb.

I had been living in the most amazing experience of personal revival and was burning to see the entire church awakened. However, in my foolishness, I was only able to sustain it for nine months. What would it look like to walk in and sustain revival over years and decades, as well as across multiple generations? Sustained revival would only come through wisdom.

It was becoming clear to me that the faith to believe "all things are possible with God" needed to be married to the Wisdom of God. I needed to understand the patterns of how He works and His character.

I dedicated myself to the special study of Proverbs. Indeed, I sometimes felt guilty for reading nothing but Proverbs in my personal Bible study. In hindsight, it was clear I kept returning to the well because I had been a great fool and was desperately in need of wisdom.

SABBATH REST

One of the topics that Fred and the prayer ministers highlighted was my inability to rest. They tied this to trusting in my own strength and ability instead of trusting in God. Somehow, in my journey of faith in God, I had managed to completely over-emphasize my own contribution. What had started in faith had quickly devolved into the force of my own will and zeal.

The next several months, Cassi and I would try to have a real Sabbath day once a week. Ironically, at first, this was the hardest day of the week. It seemed like it was easier to keep working than to rest. However, as we persisted in the discipline, eventually I started to learn how to simply rest and enjoy God's goodness.

A book that helped during this season was *The Sabbath* by Abraham Joshua Heschel.

Heschel's vision of the Sabbath as "a Cathedral in time" has informed the ongoing mission of 10 Days. We came to see 10 Days as an extended, annual opportunity for people to take a Sabbath with the Lord and enter into His rest. In fact, the lessons learned during this season even inspired the name of our first daughter—born several years later—whom we named "Sabbath."

THE HISTORY OF REVIVAL

That winter, I took a class on the history of revivals. Inspired by the class and my historic surroundings in New England, I began what has become a life-long study of moves of God throughout history.

It soon became apparent that my personal journey, from hungry seeker to revivalist to revival burnout was hardly unique. In fact, it was a pattern repeated over and over throughout history.

As I studied this subject, I gained special insight from Jonathan Edwards. Edwards was a theologian and pastor in rural New England who ministered during the First Great Awakening, a move of God that touched all thirteen American colonies in the 1730s and 40s.

In his book, Some Thoughts Concerning the Present Revival... Edwards gives a rousing defense of the First Great Awakening (1739-1742) against the "Old Lights"—a group of clergy who thought the revival was not from God. In his defense of the revival, Edwards not only documents the many incredible outcomes of the awakening, he also clearly diagnoses the excesses and errors that some proponents of the revival had committed.

"We should judge the good [of the move of God] from the bad, and not judge the whole by the parts." In other words, Edwards believed God was genuinely at work in the awakening, but that bad things were mixed in with the good.

As I read Edwards and studied the history of other revival movements, such as the Welsh Revival under Evan Roberts and the Azusa Street Revival under William Seymour, a significant pattern began to emerge, one that mapped directly onto my own experiences.

When God moved in a powerful way, it was amazing and changed everything—just as my life had been completely changed. However, because people experiencing His moving for the first time are not familiar with it and lack wisdom, they are in danger of serious and costly errors.

As I read Edwards's meticulous documentation of the errors and excesses during the First Great Awakening, it was as though he were holding a mirror to my face. My spiritual life to that point had been a case-study in the "excesses and errors" of revival.

THE EXCESSES AND ERRORS OF REVIVAL

First among Edwards's catalogue of errors was spiritual pride. Although I had feared it and endeavored rigorously to avoid it, spiritual pride was painfully evident in my journey. How could I think so much of the sacrifices I was making for the gospel? Or look down my nose at other believers who I felt were in error? Clearly, I responded to just a small amount of God's grace by having too high a view of myself and my own calling. I was guilty as charged.

Edwards also spoke of the dangers of "special revelation" or claiming to hear from God.

I didn't agree with Edwards that the Holy Spirit wasn't still speaking, or that God had not spoken to me at all over the past years. I concluded this not based on my experiences, but on the promises of Scripture. Passages like Acts 2-4, John 13-17, and 1 Corinthians 12-14 had convinced me that the New Covenant promises an intimate communion with God, and this included hearing His voice.

However, it was clear to me that many times when I thought I heard from God and had acted on my impressions, I had been grievously mistaken. I wrongly claimed, on multiple occasions, that my own thoughts or desires were God's voice. Sometimes, I even claimed what I now knew were demonic deceptions were the voice of God. In addition, at times when God was clearly speaking, I had misinterpreted what He said. Because I had never experienced supernatural signs and confirmations before, I misinterpreted legitimate encouragements God had given me.

Edwards wasn't right theologically about God not speaking today, but he was certainly right about the pitfalls of thinking you are hearing from God when what you are not hearing God's voice.

As Edwards says in conclusion, "I have seen so many instances of the failing of such impressions (of the leading of the Spirit) that would almost furnish a history." I also had seen that in my own life and in the lives of others.

MORE TYPES OF EXCESS

As his catalogue continued, Edwards warned against those who act for "short term gains while causing long term losses." He rebuked those who "work continually and never rest" and warned about "hastily introducing new things to replace the old"; something that I had been in a hurry to do.

When he saw someone with "indiscreet zeal who was too much in haste" or who "was trying to make needed changes by force instead of waiting for the Lord," he saw that as a warning sign, not a sign of God at work.

As I continued to read more of the excesses Edwards witnessed during the Great Awakening, I realized that I had personally and habitually committed every single excess and error that he wrote about.

I had been a walking embodiment of Edwards's catalogue of Revival Excess and Error.

I had spoken to other believers "with the same style and authority of Old Testament prophets," just like some in Edwards's day. I had had "inward experiences of God's grace that were nevertheless mixed." I had "been judgmental towards my fellow believers." I had "railed against and criticized prominent ministries and ministers" many times, even wanting to go and publicly rebuke them. I too, had "truly divine experiences that had 'Defects' in them," meaning that I had experiences from God that were mixed with other influences.

As I finished Edwards's book, I said to myself, "If only David and I had read this book before we set out on our journey, we could have avoided so much pain."

THE SONG OF SONGS: ENCOUNTERING THE LOVE OF GOD

In my time of healing prayer, the ministers had highlighted my need to get to know Jesus "as a gazelle"—in other words, to get to know the face of Jesus as He is revealed in the Song of Songs.

I knew in my heart this was God's word to me and responded by reading and listening to the Song of Songs over and over. To be honest, I didn't understand much of the symbolism of the book (teeth like sheep?) and even to this day I'd be hard pressed to interpret each and every detail.

However, a change began to occur as I meditated on the Song. I was beginning to see myself as the beloved of God, as someone who God loved deeply and passionately. I would experience the love and presence of God as I rested and reflected on this portion of Scripture. I was coming to know that God loved me and to see and experience some of the incredible dimensions of His love.

Prior to this time I was suspicious of people who spoke too much about the love of God. It seemed like God's love was a true but overused concept, the refuge of people who wanted "cheap grace" and weren't serious about following Jesus. I was attracted to self-sacrifice and a soldierly obedience, elements seemingly missing from western Christianity. After this season, I began to see the love of God as the thing I needed most. No longer would I consider an emphasis on God's love as soft or characteristic of compromise.

Like the woman whose journey the song chronicles, I had been "burned" in my service (Song of Songs 1:4-7). Like her, I was a failure. Now, like her, the Lord was transforming my failure into a doorway to a new kind of intimacy with him, a new way of ministering to Him and others, and a new way of following Jesus that was not about what I could do for Him but was about the unbelievable love He had for me, a love that began to fundamentally transform my very being.

I was beginning to realize I was not a Saul who God had rejected and cut off from His presence; I was His beloved.

8

"DO IT BECAUSE YOU LOVE ME" (2006)

DECEMBER, January, February—with each passing month, I was a little more whole.

In January, I kept hearing Jesus's words from John 21 over and over in my mind:

"Feed my sheep." "Tend my Lambs." "Feed my sheep."

These were the words Jesus spoke to Peter as He was restoring him to ministry. For weeks, I could not get these words out of my mind. I didn't understand what it meant at the time—they just seemed like the most beautiful words ever spoken.

Immediately after, I picked up my first ministry assignment since I had quit working for God. I began teaching a Sunday School class on prayer at my local church. It didn't occur to me at first, but finally it dawned on me: like Peter, I had "quit." Like Peter, I had gone back to my previous occupation. And like Peter, the Lord was now welcoming me back into His service with open arms.

Painful memories from my five months traveling the nation continued to hound me. Bad decisions, broken relationships, hurtful words, questions for God. Would I continue to experience these wounds for the rest of my life? Could I ever really trust God again? Would I ever be whole again?

One day, Cassi and I took a scenic drive up the Maine coastline. As we drove, unexpectedly, I found myself talking and talking, sharing everything that had happened to David and me on the trip. Cassi patiently listened as I narrated our entire five-month journey, nonstop, for seven hours. I don't think I've ever talked as much before or since. Somehow, sharing everything that happened with Cassi seemed to limit its power over me. For the first time since the first failed attempt at 10 Days, I felt like everything would be okay.

In this season, Cassi and I were hearing from God with more and more regularity through significant dreams and visions and through other believers in small prayer groups. It was profoundly impactful to have people pray over me and somehow know my innermost thoughts—things I had not shared even with Cassi. I felt seen and known by God.

In this same season, I experienced supernatural deliverance from a deep loneliness that had been part of my life since I was a child.

There was a place in the interior of my soul that was like a dark, bottomless well. It had always been there. I didn't have to go over to it, think about it, or spend time near it, but it was always there inside of me, a dark pit of loneliness.

One day, I was worshipping in the car to a song by Jason Upton. As Jason sang the lyrics, "And I don't have to fight this loneliness anymore," the bottomless, lonely place in my soul disappeared in a moment, never to return. I thought I would struggle with this loneliness every day for the rest of my life. Unexpectedly, God delivered me in an instant.

With this gone, I felt as though I could truly rest. "I could see living like this for a very long time," I said to myself. I felt living forever, one day at a time, would be an unspeakable delight.

In March, our first son Gabriel was born, changing our entire world and filling our lives with joy. God, in His mercy, was restoring all we had lost—in fact, He was making things better than they had ever been.

"DO IT BECAUSE YOU LOVE ME"

After Gabriel's birth, 10 Days Pentecost was coming up fast, the one-year anniversary of my crash. I had taken Fred's advice to do the 10 Days "small and simple." We would do it with my Sunday School class at church. No cold-calling hundreds of churches. No traveling around the nation for five months. No 24/7 prayer. We would just try to have a daily prayer gathering with a few people for 10 Days leading up to the Global Day of Prayer on Pentecost Sunday.

However, as we approached 10 Days, I was petrified.

I told the Lord, "Last time I did this it took me nine months to recover—what is going to happen to me this time?"

It was understandable that I felt this way, and yet as I asked God this question, I felt I needed to repent of accusation toward Him in my heart. As I apologized, He spoke to me clearly.

"Last time you did 10 Days because you wanted something."

As I heard those words in my spirit, I knew exactly what He meant. I had done it because I wanted to see sweeping revival in America. I was willing to give my all, to sacrifice everything to reach that goal. And yet, the end of it had been disaster, and revival had not come.

"This time," He said, "do it because you love Me."

As those words crashed over me like waves, I saw in my mind's eye the image of a gazelle, leaping over the mountains, coming quickly towards me.

In the Song of Songs, the gazelle leaping over the mountains is symbolic of the return of Jesus. He is coming quickly for His beloved Bride, just as it says in the book of Revelation. Jonathan Edwards interpreted the gazelle leaping over the mountains as the coming of revival when God's people resolve to patiently seek Him. I knew God was saying that if I would seek Him in this new way, because I love Him, that He would come quickly. Revival would come in the near term, and finally, the Lord would return.

A SMALL SUCCESS

A few days later, stronger and wiser than we were in 2005, we hosted our first successful 10 Days at our local church. Rather than 24/7 prayer, we had two to four hours of prayer each day. Rather than trying to get an entire city, we had two to seven people in the prayer room at any point in time. While the numbers were not huge, God's presence was powerful. People who were hungry for more of God came every day and were changed in His presence.

10 Days took place while Cassi and I were in the middle of a move. Our winter rental was up, but because of the high cost of living in our area, it was hard for us to find a place we could afford. The uncertainty around our living situation continued into 10 Days. We had to move but had nowhere to go, and Cassi soon found herself with a bad case of strep throat brought on by the stress of our situation.

It was June 2, our fifth wedding anniversary, and although Cassi couldn't talk or swallow food due to the infection, we were at the church for prayer. That evening, as I walked and prayed in another room holding Gabriel, The Spirit of the Lord spoke to Cassi and told her that He was about to heal her of strep throat. About five seconds after she heard those words from the Holy Spirit, she felt heat on her throat. Immediately, the pain was gone and she could speak and swallow normally. She's never had strep throat again.

That night, we celebrated God's work with a steak dinner for our anniversary, a meal that would have been impossible without the miracle. Sometimes, when God does a miracle, it's important to eat steak. The day after 10 Days ended, we found ourselves in a new apartment that fit our budget and was ideally situated between work and school commitments.

For the first time, we hosted a successful 10 Day prayer gathering. Cities hadn't stopped, but a small group of people had prayed a lot more than usual. In response, God had moved and done miracles. And, in what felt like a major victory, my life had not fallen apart this time.

This time, I had done 10 Days because I loved Him, not to get something I wanted. God had responded with His presence, healed my wife, and set us in a new home.

9

SEEDS OF TRANSFORMATION (2006)

IN 2006, I met Jeff Marks. Jeff led a ministry called New England Concerts of Prayer. His ministry focused on uniting believers in the six-states of Massachusetts, Vermont, New Hampshire, Maine, Rhode Island, and Connecticut to pray for revival and awakening. Before I met Jeff I had been praying God would lead me to a mentor. I thought it was a hopeless prayer—I didn't know anyone who did what I was called to do, or so I thought. At the same time, Jeff had been praying to find someone to mentor so he could pass on what he had learned. We were an answer to each other's prayers.

That summer, Jeff invited me to The Institute for Campus Revival and Awakening, hosted at Yale University. This conference occurred annually for three years and would play a significant role in the early formation of 10 Days.

I was excited to go to Yale. It was Jonathan Edwards's alma mater and home to his original manuscripts. One of the world's leading Edwards scholars would be speaking at the Institute. However, while I enjoyed learning more about the great man, two other speakers would be more impactful for the future of 10 Days.

TALES OF TRANSFORMATION

George Otis Jr., leader of The Sentinel Group and producer of the Transformations documentary series was one of the keynote speakers. Although jet-lagged and groggy after a sleepless flight from the South Pacific, his testimonies of transforming revival in the Fiji islands were almost unbelievable.

These villagers were seeing incredible miracles take place: people were healed, the dead were raised; even the very earth itself, both land and water, was restored by the power of God. Otis described what was happening outside the western church as "the events of the Book of Acts—plus." These people were seemingly doing the "greater works" that Jesus promised in John 14:12.

FIRE FROM HEAVEN

Otis shared an unbelievable testimony from a village that had gone through great difficulty. Their coral reef, on which they depended for survival, had died and all the fish had left. On land, wild pigs had come and rooted up all their yams and other foods. They were low on food and in danger of starvation. Most concerning, hopelessness, violence, and suicide were running rampant among the children and teens.

Amid this desperate situation, a group called the "Healing the Land" team was invited to come and help. Their name came from 2 Chronicles 7:14, "If my people who are called by my name will humble themselves, and pray, and seek my face, and turn from their wicked ways then I will hear from Heaven, I will forgive their sins, and I will heal their land."

George shared how westerners took "Healing the Land" to mean "saving people," but the Fijians saw "healing the land" as holistic, including the earth, animal life, the water, and the people who lived on the land. This was a more biblical view as Jesus is not just the rightful ruler of "all people" but of "all creation."

As a tribal people, the chief would set the agenda for what was happening, and everyone would follow his lead. So, when the chief invited the twenty or so members of the Healing the Land team to come and serve, the village responded. Three daily times of prayer and repentance were coupled with house-to-house ministry and fasting. Everyone was exhorted to get rid of their idols, and broken relationships were mended. This season of consecration led to a breakthrough so extraordinary I struggled to believe it was true.

George recounted how, in response to this season of prayer and repentance, a ball of fire descended from the sky. It first burned over the sea, then moved into the area of the dead coral reef. This visible ball of fire was seen first by a woman whose son had committed suicide, and then by hundreds in the village as it hovered over the waters, causing an incredible churning. It was like the pillar of fire that the Israelites saw in the wilderness.

When the ball lifted back out of the water and returned to the sky, it was immediately evident the coral reef had come back to life. Fish returned instantly and in greater numbers than ever; villagers were able to walk out and harvest fish with buckets because of the abundance.

I had never heard anything like this. It was the most incredible miracle story I had ever heard.

I was also struck by George's observation that "the book of Acts—plus" phenomena were occurring in many nations of the world, but not in the western, developed world. I knew in my heart that God had given me 10 Days to see just this kind of transformation, not only in tribal nations, but also in the west. This testimony opened my eyes to the possibilities of what God could do through prayer and repentance.

Another speaker at this event was Lou Engle, founder of The Call, a movement hosting massive prayer meetings in stadiums. Lou shared how he had done a forty-day water fast that year, and how the Lord had responded to his fast in miraculous ways. Lou's testimony stirred something in me:

"I'd love to do a forty-day water fast," I thought to myself. It seemed impossible, and yet so biblical. If we were called to do the works of Jesus, why not start by doing the fast of Jesus?

I returned from the Institute with dreams of transforming revival in my heart and a determination to do a forty-day fast.

THE FAST

I knew from my visionary experience in 2004 that God wanted 10 Days to be a global movement where entire cities would stop for prayer and repentance. From my failures in 2005 and the wise counsel of others, I now understood that this would not take place in one year but was something that God would do over time. God had shown me the end goal, the place we were heading together, but the walking out the vision had to be accomplished step by careful step.

That fall, I led another Sunday School class focused on prayer at my local church. As a culminating activity, I invited our class to fast during the Ten Days of Awe. Inspired by Lou Engle, like so many before and since, I resolved to do a forty-day water fast, culminating with the 10 Days. There was just one little problem with my plan to fast like Jesus. By this point, it must be painfully obvious that my wife is a complete saint for putting up with me. She wisely felt working to support our family, serving in ministry, going to school full-time, and having a newborn, would not go well with a forty-day water fast. I listened to her counsel and decided to do a forty-day liquid (juice) fast instead.

The fast was one of the hardest things I had ever attempted. Aside from the physical difficulty, I felt all alone. After five days, I confessed to a friend "I just don't think I can do this on my own. I need other believers to be fasting with me."

The next Monday, he forwarded me an email—JHOP Boston, a prayer ministry in Boston founded by Lou Engle, had called a forty-day fast with the exact same start and end dates as my fast. I was not alone after all. Pushed forward by this encouragement, I kept going.

As we moved into the final ten days of the fast, I was joined by seven people in the Sunday School class of my local church. We were doing what God had showed me in a small way. Cities were not stopping, but seven people were fasting and praying during the fall 10 Days. It was a small but significant step.

TWO TRANSFORMING ENCOUNTERS WITH GOD

During the final ten days of the fast, I had two significant encounters in prayer.

For as long as I could remember, I had struggled with pride. I thought I was better than other people. At the same time, there was a strong insecurity associated with it. Because I recognized this tendency in myself, I had often tried to combat it by building a wall around it, keeping myself out of leadership or other situations that might somehow fuel my pride. Honestly, I didn't trust myself in this area of besetting sin.

One evening as I prayed on our couch, had a strong mental picture, like a movie that began playing out in my mind's eye.

In the vision, Jesus was on the earth, walking around like one of us. I saw the Lord Jesus walking through the green, sunny countryside with His inner circle of best friends. They were talking and laughing, enjoying themselves. I was not part of His inner circle. Instead, I was doing a rather menial job, I was responsible for picking apples in an orchard. I was a lowly "migrant farm worker" in the Kingdom of God.

In the experience, I immediately noticed that I experienced no jealousy or envy. In normal life, I would have felt jealous and deeply insecure that I wasn't one of Jesus's inner circle and instead had a seemingly insignificant role. But in the vision, I felt peaceful and content with the amazing job that I had as an apple picker. Honestly, I was just honored to catch a glimpse of Jesus and His friends. As I realized I was free from any jealousy and was enjoying the feeling of freedom, I looked to my left and there was Jesus, smiling at me and picking apples with me. The scene shifted to a dining room table. Jesus and His inner circle of twelve to fifteen were having dinner together, sitting around the table, enjoying themselves. In this vision, I was one of the waiters serving their party. I brought in one of the apples I had picked and presented it to the group as part of the meal.

Once again, I experienced no jealousy or insecurity at being outside the inner circle. I simply felt honored that I could be so close to Jesus and His best friends. It was an honor to serve them.

Since then, I have not struggled with pride as I did before. It's not that I'm perfect or have never felt insecurity, jealousy, envy, or pride. Now it's more of a passing emotion that doesn't have power over me. The Spirit of God set me free.

CALL 120

Several nights later, I had a second profound encounter that would direct the trajectory of 10 Days over the next year.

As I was praying late one night, I heard the Lord say, "Call 120 to pray for 10 Days leading up to Pentecost."

I heard this so clearly and immediately wrote it down. "Is this for this year, or for some point in the future?" I wondered.

As the experience continued, the Lord showed me a church building that had four "rooms of prayer." The rooms were named "Worship,"

"Intercession," "Scripture," and "Silence." I saw people inside this church building (it was my local church) moving from room to room, praying in four different ways. After the vision ended, I wrote it all down in detail.

The Ten Days of Awe ended, and we celebrated with a meal together. There were only seven of us who joined in 10 Days that fall, but every person who did the fast had a testimony of how God had moved in their life. It was remarkable to me how consistent God was to show up whenever people sought him. After forty days, I was beyond thrilled to be eating again.

After the fast was over, one of my coworkers, noting that I was eating once again, asked me, "Did you find what you were looking for?"

"Yes," I said. I had found it. I had my next step.

10

NORTHFIELD (2007)

I HAD learned so much since the crash: sabbath rest, the wisdom of Proverbs, and lessons from the history of revival. Most importantly, I was learning to walk intimately with God as His beloved. As I embarked on a new, larger adventure, it was time to put what I had learned into action.

Instead of just pondering God's direction to "call 120" on my own as I had done in 2005, I immediately sought wise counsel regarding the timing and location of what I had heard. I had specific questions. In my vision, the four rooms were at my local church. Was it supposed to be there? Or was that just incidental to the experience? The biggest question was timing. Was the vision for the upcoming Pentecost, or for the future?

In contrast to previous years, I wanted it to be for the future. I had learned that following Jesus always carries a cost. I wanted to be obedient above all, but if the choice was easier obedience, I'd take that.

Previously, I wanted to do hard things to prove to myself and others that I was a real disciple. Now, I knew who I was and who I was following. I also knew the road ahead would be hard enough on its own. I was not looking for additional difficulty.

As I shared this word with my mentor, Jeff Marks, God touched him powerfully.

"We need to do it this year." He was adamant.

Jeff was part of a nascent network of New England leaders who were uniting the church for revival in our region. This network included many prominent ministry leaders from Boston and beyond. He shared with me their plan to host a regional Global Day of Prayer event on Pentecost Sunday. This 10 Days of Prayer with 120 people could be part of the larger effort.

I sought the advice of my aunt, who confirmed I should move forward right away and encouraged me not to be passive or fearful. Wise counsel confirmed God had not yet revealed the location of the event. I had seen the vision in a familiar place, but most probably He had another spot picked out.

NOW, A LITTLE LARGER

God was now moving 10 Days out of a small and simple expression into something larger, something that would touch the entire region. It was still much smaller than "cities stopping" around the world, but it was a leap forward. Most importantly, I wanted to see what happened when a group of people stopped everything to seek the Lord. If I was going to trumpet this to the nations, I needed to know first-hand that it worked.

Mobilizing an event for 120 people was a stretch. My one attempt to organize a large 10 Days of Prayer had been a failure. However, this time I was determined to walk in faith, not trust in my zeal or self-sacrifice to make it happen. My confidence was that if God had said to do it, God would provide for it. I was hanging everything upon His word.

Knowing my own frailty and need for God, I resolved to take a half-day for prayer each week to listen to Him and pray for the project.

THE NEW ENGLAND ALLIANCE

That winter, Jeff invited me to attend one of the first meetings of the New England Alliance. I was amazed to meet so many people who carried my heart for unity in the church, and for revival and awakening. I had no idea there were so many like-minded people in the New England region.

Through the Alliance, I joined up with the Global Day of Prayer New England team. Like St. Louis in 2005, I would lead the 10 Days of Prayer effort, while the rest of the team focused on bringing thousands of people together for a large event on the Global Day of Prayer.

These new connections were encouraging. However, for 10 Days to become a reality, I prayed desperately for my two greatest needs.

"Lord, show me where to host the event and send someone to help me."

A WELL-TIMED PHONE CALL

It was a cold Saturday morning in February. That morning, as I began work on a paper on Jonathan Edwards and the first great awakening, I received a voice message from Al Shimer. Al and I were working together on the Global Day of Prayer.

Al's message was about a man from western Massachusetts named David McCahon. Apparently, David was interested in helping with the upcoming 10 Days.

David lived in the same area where Jonathan Edwards had ministered, the part of New England I was writing about at that very moment. Al also mentioned something about a historic campus founded by Evangelist D.L. Moody.

Edwards I knew and loved. But D.L. Moody? I knew he was from Chicago, but what did D.L. Moody have to do with western Massachusetts? I was about to learn more than I could have imagined.

A MOST AMAZING STORY

A few minutes later, David and I were on the phone. I quickly learned that he was a pastor, a prayer and unity guy, and a historian. On top of that, he wanted to help with 10 Days of Prayer. So far, so good.

And then he told me a most amazing story.

That very morning, he had opened the newspaper and learned that the Northfield campus was planning a ten-day camp based on the TV show American Idol.

David explained to me how Northfield was founded by Evangelist D.L. Moody in 1879 as a school for girls. Moody and His wife were buried there. The campus Moody founded was currently up for sale for forty million dollars. And the American Idol camp would be performing right next to the graves of Mr. and Mrs. D.L. Moody.

When David found out about the camp, he was grieved. "American IDOL...at Northfield...for ten days?" he remarked to his wife Cindy. "Moody must be rolling in his grave."

After some conciliatory words from his wife, David prayed a little prayer.

"Lord, I wish you would do your own ten-day thing at Northfield." Those exact words.

Thirty minutes after that short prayer, Al Shimer called David. The two men had not spoken in more than five years. Al told David about the vision of 10 Days of Prayer leading up to the Global Day of Prayer. He also shared how we were still looking for a location and that I needed some serious help.

"Would you be willing to help this young guy pray for 10 Days?" Al asked.

"Help him? Are you kidding? I'm in. And I already know where we are going to do it."

I had been praying for God to give us a location and to send someone to help me. God had answered both prayers at once.

NORTHFIELD

As we continued to talk, David shared more about the history of Northfield. His passion for the righteous roots of New England's history was contagious.

I knew a little about D.L. Moody, mostly from his years in Chicago. He was the Billy Graham of the 1800s, a famous evangelist who won tens of thousands to Christ all over the world.

David explained to me how Moody had started two high schools in western Massachusetts in the last twenty years of his life, one for girls and one for boys: Northfield and Mt. Hermon.

He would also host large summer conferences at the schools. People came from around the world to attend the Northfield Conferences. The most famous of them was in 1886, when a gathering of over 200 college students launched the Student Volunteer Movement. Amazingly, SVM would send more than 20,000 missionaries overseas in just thirty-five years. To put that number in context, until 1886, the United States had sent less than 2,000 missionaries overseas in its entire history. Hundreds of millions of modern Christians in Africa, South America, and Asia could trace their spiritual lineage back to SVM and Northfield.

David shared how in the 1930s, the schools began to depart from following Jesus. Within a few decades, they were both just typical elite and expensive New England prep schools.

In 1986, on the 100th anniversary of the birth of the Student Volunteer Movement, he attended an international gathering of mission leaders at Northfield-Mt. Hermon. Ever since then, for twenty-one years, David had been praying for the two campuses; especially Northfield, to return to their righteous roots and to be used for the glory of God once again.

In 2005, NMH announced they would consolidate their students to the Mt. Hermon campus and seek to sell the Northfield campus. The asking price was forty million dollars.

David was thrilled Northfield was for sale and was asking God to provide a Christian buyer who would return the property to its original intention.

DAVID AND JONATHAN

After this auspicious phone introduction, we met in person several weeks later at the Northfield campus. I got my car stuck in the snow, and David helped push me it out—a fitting initial action for our friendship. David was twenty-six years my senior. He had a kind face with grey-white hair, a white beard, and an easy laugh. This was the second "David" I would partner closely with. Apparently, the Lord enjoyed having David and Jonathan together.

The Northfield campus was enchanting, like something out of a storybook. Each building was unique, some of them having spires, turrets, clocks and other whimsical design features. The campus was massive, with dozens of large, beautiful buildings and remarkable views of the surrounding mountains, river, and countryside. And yet, this beautiful campus built for thousands of people to inhabit was entirely empty. We were the only people there in the middle of the day.

As we walked the pathways, I was reminded of Isaiah's prophecy that "desolate cities" would be inhabited once again. I had never seen a desolate city before, but the prayer certainly seemed to fit Northfield.

After our initial meeting, David and I reached out to Northfield-Mt. Hermon, and began to talk to them about renting one of the buildings for May. Step by step, the vision was coming together.

WORKING WITH GOD

One the biggest revival errors I made prior to my burnout experience, was "trying to make needful changes by force instead of waiting on God."

Frustrated when people didn't respond immediately, I had often tried to force people to do things I thought God wanted us to do. When they dug in their heels even more, I became offended, angry, and wounded.

Painful experience had taught me this was a horrible strategy. My new plan was to share what I thought God wanted to do with as many people as possible, allow everyone the freedom to decide how to respond, and trust God for the result. I could be passionate about what God was doing and give people the opportunity to take part without coercion. It wasn't enough to work for God, now I was determined to learn how to work with God at every step.

David and I began inviting people to join in the 10 Days of Prayer, and people responded. Using various networks and email lists, the word began to get out and people started registering from all over the nation. While we weren't approaching 120 registered to live on campus for 10 Days, at least we had some people responding and a verbal agreement to rent a building at Northfield.

In the meantime, my weekly, half-day prayer walks were essential to staying in a place of faith and encouragement. On one such walk, I brought up an issue to the Lord that really troubled me. Because of the cost of renting the facility, we had to charge a fee for people to join the 10 Days.

I told the Lord, "You should not have to pay in order to pray."

The Lord responded, "I want those who come to pay a cost because together you will be to Me like the woman who broke a vial of perfume at My feet. That is why you have to pay."

My heart melted. The thought that we could move His heart in that way, to touch the heart of the King—what a tremendous honor. On another occasion, the Lord spoke to me out of Zechariah chapter 6, a rather obscure passage about a special offering taken to make "Yeshua" the high priest a crown.

"What you are doing will be like the offering of Heldai, Tobijah, and Jedaiah. You are making me a crown. The crown will be a reminder in my temple to those who give to make it."

I was beginning to realize this time would be very special to the Lord. David and I, along with 120 others, would have the honor of giving an extravagant offering to the King of Kings. This 10 Days was going to be something that King Jesus would remember and cherish. The thought of touching His heart was now motivating me far more than results. I was learning to be led by love.

As happened with the woman who anointed Jesus with perfume, there was some misunderstanding about this extravagant offering. Some good friends wanted to use 10 Days primarily to mobilize prayer regarding the gay marriage issue, a hot button topic at the time.

"It'd be easier to get people to come and pray about the current crisis...."

While I deeply cared about this issue, the Lord was clearly calling us to give a love offering to Him, not mobilize intercession against gay marriage. There would always be needs, crises, causes, and injustices. However, the heart of our gathering had to be what God had showed me in 2006: "Do it because you love me."

A DEVASTATING SETBACK, A STUNNING REVELATION

A month before the 10 Days of Prayer was to begin, I received the worst news I could imagine from the owners of Northfield.

Our verbal agreement to rent a building on campus was off. They didn't trust us and were pulling the plug on our gathering.

I received the email while I was in between classes at seminary. I was stunned.

I told the Lord, "How can this be happening? You've given us so many signs. I know you want us to pray there."

The bad news was so upsetting, it seemed to short-circuit my system. I promptly passed out on a couch and fell asleep.

When I woke up an hour later, I sensed the presence of God around me. Immediately, I picked up my laptop and composed a humble reply.

I apologized for anything we might have done wrong and stressed that I valued the relationship more than just the specific outcome of hosting the event. Maybe we could work together in the future, and if not, I was sending gratitude and blessing their way.

Within a few minutes, I received a reply thanking me for my email, and informing me that we were back on. Phew. And Praise God. As I had learned from studying the Proverbs, a humble answer had turned away wrath. God had rescued us from disaster.

And on the other side of near disaster, came an incredible breakthrough.

A few days later, I received a second email from NMH. One of their staff wanted to share a document with us. I had no idea what to expect.

As I opened the attachment, I found a letter written in the year 1880 by D.L. Moody entitled "A Call to Believers."[1] The letter was an invitation to come to Northfield for ten days of prayer based on Acts

1 See Appendix.

Chapter 1; exactly what we were returning there to do. Once again, I was stunned to silence.

When my speech returned, I called David. "I don't know what this means, but this is God. We are really onto something here."

After researching the letter further, we discovered this 1880 ten days of prayer in Northfield was the first Northfield Conference. Just six years before the Student Volunteer Movement was birthed, these world-famous summer conferences began with ten days of prayer. At the end of the 1880 Northfield ten day prayer gathering, the first building on campus was dedicated to God.

Northfield had started in a ten day prayer meeting based on Acts 1 and 2. Now, 126 years later, the campus was for sale. And God had brought a bunch of misfits back to unknowingly do exactly what they did when the campus was founded. Somehow, we had stumbled into something big.

LIKE THE SONS OF ZADOK

On the night I received the 10 Days vision, I had warned the Lord, "No one is going to want to stop everything for 10 Days to pray and repent."

In fact, it was even harder than I expected to get people to stop everything to pray for 10 Days. While I had high hopes we'd have 120 people living on site and stopping everything, we ended up with just fifteen to twenty who committed at that level. Many others would come and go as they were able, living off-site and commuting in to pray. This wasn't all I hoped for and yet clearly God was with us even if it did not look exactly as I initially thought.

As we approached 10 Days, I sensed God speaking to us out of a very obscure passage, Ezekiel 44.

This passage speaks of the sons of Zadok who minister to the Lord and not to men. Because of our God-given focus on ministering to the Lord and offering Him an extravagant offering, this passage really resonated.

There are very specific instructions given to the sons of Zadok. For instance, they do not have shaved heads or long hair, but close-cropped hair. They do not drink wine when they go to minister. They cannot touch a dead person unless it is a child, a wife, or close family member, and then they must wait seven days before they minister to the Lord.

Obviously, these special instructions do not apply to us as New Testament believers. However, as a prophetic act, I decided to do several of these acts of consecration seven days before 10 Days would begin. I would trim my long hair short, avoid wine, and consecrate myself to minister to the Lord.

As we arrived at the beginning of this time of consecration, tragedy struck our family. Cassi was pregnant again with our second child. Just seven days before the 10 Days was to begin, she miscarried.

I was angry at the devil and even somehow blamed myself for what happened. However, in contrast to 2005, I was not shaken in my relationship with God. Here we were, at the threshold of this God-breathed season, and the enemy was killing our children. Bizarrely, I found myself following these ancient, priestly guidelines to the letter, including the rules for losing a family member. As with the first miscarriage, I cut my long hair. However, this time I did not shave it, but close cropped it.

Following Jesus was hard, and the pain was strong as it had been in 2005. However, this time was different. In the midst of our loss, we set ourselves apart to minister to the Lord.

WATERS ABOVE, WATERS BELOW

As 10 Days began, we made the beautiful two-hour drive to Northfield. As we descended into the river valley where Northfield is located, I heard this from the Lord:

"The Waters above will combine with the waters below and create a great flood that will cover the earth."

This was a reference to the flood of Noah, but God seemed to be speaking of a flood of His glory that was coming soon on the Earth.

Immediately, I felt the "waters above" had to do with our prayers that we were praying now and that the "waters below" spoke to the prayers of the Saints of old, prayers that were still speaking. The flood was a Habakkuk 2:14 flood, that "the knowledge of the glory of the Lord will cover the earth as waters cover the Sea."

God was bringing us to Northfield, a historic well of revival, because He was bringing together the prayers of the Saints, past and present, to cover the earth in a flood of the glory of God.

"YOUR PEOPLE ARE WEIRD"

As we launched into 10 Days, I had a nervous feeling in the pit of my stomach. I had only the faintest outline of a plan. If God didn't show up, this entire thing would be a disaster. He had faithfully brought us here, step by step. Now, I needed Him to come through when it mattered most.

In obedience to the vision, we had set aside four rooms: a worship room, an intercessory "boiler room" in the basement, a "silence" room, and a "Scripture" room. The worship room was the main room where all the forms of prayer converged. We decided against doing 24/7 prayer, and instead had four prayer watches of three hours each from six a.m. to six p.m. plus a two-hour evening service. Everyone was asked to be part of six hours of prayer during the day plus the evening sessions. In the remaining time, people could rest, but we also had various clean-up, cooking and other chores that we asked our participants to help with. We were all there to serve and pray together. In all these arrangements, we were trying our best to live out the original vision of "stopping everything" for an extended season of prayer.

As the first evening began, I was pulled away from worship and prayer to care for Cassi and little Gabe. The last week had been incredibly hard, and I wanted to make sure they were okay. After getting them settled in our bedroom, I returned to the prayer room.

When I returned to the room, our group of about forty seemed to have descended into total chaos. As I entered the room, a large black woman in a bandana was rolling back and forth on the floor.

"I've read about this," I thought. "This is holy rolling."

My eyes glanced to the right, where a red-haired woman was sitting on the ground and laughing like a hyena.

"That must be holy laughter." I thought, clinically. I had read about it but never seen it happen.

My immediate instinct was to put a stop to all of this and bring us back to "order." My mentor, Jeff Marks, was the one who was laying hands and anointing everyone with oil, which apparently was causing all of the insanity. Clearly, he would not be much help.

"Where's David?" I asked myself, getting desperate.

I found David lying on the ground, his face glazed over with a blissful expression.

I quickly diagnosed his condition: "That's being slain in the Spirit." I had read about that too.

Clearly, David wasn't going to ride to my rescue.

Everyone in the room could see I was uncomfortable with what was happening. I wanted to see the Bible come to life, but this just seemed strange. Of course, I had heard about all these things but never seen them in real life. I had never been in leadership where these types of manifestations were happening. In fact, the largest prayer group I had ever led was about ten people. If I had been more confident, I might have shut everything down. Thankfully, I was ignorant and insecure. I had no idea what to do, so I did nothing.

That night, as I went to bed, I found myself thinking about all the strange things that had happened that night and laughing with the Lord.

"Your people are weird," I told Him. "But I like them."

SIGNS

After a memorable opening night, I woke up and prepared to lead the 9 a.m. to noon prayer time. With a ten-minute window before we started, I ducked into one of the other prayer rooms for some quiet time with the Lord. I opened my Bible at random to Isaiah 26 and 27, stopping at Is. 27:3.

"In that day, sing to her. A vineyard of red wine. I the LORD keep it, I water it every moment lest any hurt it. I keep it night and day."

As we began the prayer time, an older woman, Ethel Doolittle, who had prayed over thirty years for God to revive Moody's legacy at Northfield, felt it would be appropriate to start the prayer gathering with the motto given to the school by D.L. Moody himself. The motto was from Isaiah 27:3 "I the LORD keep it, I water it every moment lest any hurt it. I will keep it night and day."

My jaw dropped to the floor. Somehow my random Bible study at our first morning on campus had ended right on the school's motto. Clearly, God was watching over this place. And, somehow, history kept coming alive before our eyes.

A TASTE OF JOHN 17

As the first several days rolled along, something incredible and difficult to describe was happening. We were experiencing a tangible measure of what Jesus prayed for in John 17. Supernatural love and unity in the Spirit had been poured out on us. God had dropped a taste of John 17 unity on our gathering. While at future 10 Days events, we would teach about this reality, there was no teaching of any kind at this event. People didn't know the backstory, or how important John 17 was to the overall vision. In fact, even I was slow to realize we were experiencing an answer to those early prayers.

Our core group was diverse denominationally and ethnically, and was from various economic backgrounds. And yet, all of us noticed the unusual love for one another and unity that God was pouring out. We began talking about it as something we could protect and guard and thinking about how we could honor one another above ourselves. Love and good deeds flowed naturally from this place and all our conversation seemed to be focused on the Lord. Something incredible was happening.

As we were experiencing this unusual grace, I finally began to recollect those early experiences in Santa Fe. 10 Days had been borne out of asking God how I could be part of Jesus receiving the answer to His prayer in John 17. Somehow, God was releasing grace for Jesus's prayer to actually be answered, and we were the beneficiaries.

For years I had marveled at Jesus's words, "Let them be one just as we are one." How could human beings experience the type of union that the Father and Son experience with one another? But now, we were not just reading about it, we were experiencing a measure of it firsthand. This was something else altogether—it was like heaven on earth.

WHAT DOES JOHN 17 FEEL LIKE?

I like testimonies that can be easily communicated. Healings are like that—someone has a broken bone, people pray, and it is healed. This is very easy to talk about. On the other hand, it's difficult to describe what it is like to experience John 17 unity. I'll do my best.

First of all, it's something inside of you and it's also something around you, in the air. It's in you and it's in the atmosphere. This lines up with Jesus's words in John 17:22 about the key role that His glory plays in unity. His glory is within us through the Holy Spirit, but also all around us.

This experience of glory is between you and God vertically, but it's also between you and other people horizontally. It's the presence of God experienced vertically and horizontally at the same time.

It feels like all you can think about or talk about is Jesus. During those times, one of the things I noticed was that what we often consider normal conversation was almost non-existent. God was doing so much and people could not stop talking about Him.

I was completely surprised by the inner experience of my heart and mind. "Why do I irrationally love these people?" I kept asking myself. And yet, I did love them, deeply and from the heart.

It was almost traumatic to move from this dynamic experience of love and glory into what we often call normal life. I had to run out for supplies at one point during the 10 Days; the routine act of going to a local drugstore felt painful. I'd compare it to culture shock—what I had previously considered normal now seemed like spiritual oppression and darkness that was almost too much to bear. In the future, I would learn to carry what I was experiencing along with me, but those initial experiences were a look into the darkness of our world that we simply accept.

Finally, John 17 manifesting resulted in all kinds of love, good deeds, and miracles in the community. There were too many amazing things happening around us to record it all, but our love for one another was foundational, like a basin that was holding all that God was pouring out on us.

I have never been the same since this experience.

SIMPLY PRAY...THEN GOD

All we were doing was praying and praising God, using the "four rooms" model of worship, intercession, Scripture reading, and silence. We started at six a.m. each day, and prayed until six p.m., took a break for dinner, and gathered again at seven p.m. for a corporate session with everyone joining together in the evening. There was no preaching or teaching; it was just us talking to God and God talking to us. In addition to our core group of people living on site, new folks were driving in each day to join us. Our prayer room had become a hive of regional activity, with many coming to see and experience what God was doing.

As we entered each prayer time with openness to the Spirit's leading, I was struck by how each session was completely different. There was no way to predict at the beginning where we'd end up. God took over, and each prayer set was totally new.

I was beginning to understand the God who created billions of galaxies and endless diversity of plant and animal life. I had known Him as the One who never changes, but now I was getting to know Him as the God who is always doing a new thing, the God who is endlessly creative and forever fascinating.

And, while I was struggling with some of the weird things that would happen under the power of the Holy Spirit, I was also beginning to experience some of the benefits. For instance, I had always been very skeptical about the idea of "holy laughter." And yet, I began to experience an unspeakable and glorious joy inside of me. And when I experienced it, I would laugh! While I tried to be skeptical, the experience was clean, refreshing, and glorious—it felt good, made God seem real, and made problems seem small.

In this atmosphere, supernatural activity exploded. Tracking what God was doing was like counting raindrops in a downpour. One notable miracle was a healing from terminal pancreatic cancer. I don't even remember us praying for the woman who was sick, but she felt a change while we were there. When she went home and visited the doctors, she was entirely cancer free. She went from having a few months to live to continuing cancer free at the time of this writing.

One of our core group, Steven, was a banker. About seven days in, Steve told me he was counting all the attendees. Of course, the thought had never entered my mind.

"I think God is going to bring 120 people just like he told you" Steven said.

I was entirely focused on getting 120 people to stop everything for all 10 Days. It had never occurred to me that what God told me could apply to all attendees and not just to people taking all 10 Days for prayer. But what Steven said made sense. On our final day, as we prepared to leave Northfield for the Global Day of Prayer event, Steven gave me our final total. Exactly 122 people had come to be part of 10 Days. "Call 120" had happened, just as the Lord told had said.

AFTERMATH AND NEXT STEPS

The Global Day of Prayer was good. Five thousand people gathered for a prayer meeting in the middle of the state. Honestly, I was too exhausted from 10 Days to participate much in the large event. As in 2005, I had given absolutely everything I had to the Lord and to His people. However, this time the result was completely different. My only regret was that I didn't have more to give.

As I left the 2007 10 Days of Prayer, my relationship with God was completely changed. Nothing would ever be the same again.

My faith had grown exponentially. The combination of experiencing God's presence, with the Scripture, in community, with powerful signs and miracles confirming God was with us made a few things clear to me. God was alive and I could trust the Bible. I didn't just believe it intellectually; I knew it deep down in my bones. Doubts that had plagued me for years now seemed small. The apologetic of God's powerful, undeniable presence completely overwhelmed my skeptical mind.

John 17 Unity was no longer just a theory, an unbelievable prayer of Jesus. It was now something I had experienced.

I found myself gripped as never before by the mission of the church—to bring the gospel to every nation, tribe, and language. God's desire to be known among the nations had become my deep heart desire as well.

I was growing rapidly in charismatic experiences like hearing God's voice. It was incredible how in environments charged by extraordinary prayer, I would hear from God so much more often and frequently.

Finally, 10 Days Northfield was proof of concept that this actually worked. Taking 10 Days off from normal life to worship, pray, and repent was changing lives. And I was not only the purveyor of this message, I had been personally transformed. Incredible unity was experienced, the heavy presence of God surrounded everything, lives were changed, and miracles were normal.

It was still incredibly hard to get anyone to take 10 Days off to pray, but those who said "yes" had their lives turned upside down.

FROM CATALYTIC SEASON TO REGULAR RHYTHM

The other side of 10 Days was hard.

I was physically and emotionally exhausted from those intense times of prayer. Pouring out everything before God comes with a cost and as I landed back in normal life, I was at a deficit. After what we experienced, so called "normal life" was no longer normal. It felt like hell compared to where I had been living, in a worship saturated environment full of the presence of God. I was having a hard time adjusting, like a diver who comes up from the depths too quickly. I had grown used to a measure of the glory of God all around me and with it taken away, life was almost unbearable. I was also worried about going back to the way I was before, that my personal transformation would be fleeting.

One night, just a few days after getting back, I was complaining about this to my wife. Having had enough of my lament, she told me, "Take the baby, get out of the house, and go find a prayer meeting."

"She's being so unreasonable," I said to myself as I pushed the stroller down the streets of our town. How was I supposed to find a prayer meeting in our small town? I barely knew anyone here.

As I walked, I felt the Holy Spirit say, "Go to Brian Barry's house."

I knew Brian as a classmate in seminary. We had talked several times but we weren't close friends. I also knew that he lived in a larger apartment building in town, but did not know which apartment was his. With nothing else to go on, I walked about a mile from my home to Brian's building.

As I arrived, I ran into a stranger coming out of the house.

"Do you know where Brian Barry lives?" I asked.

She pointed me to his door, the first one on the right.

As I approached the door, the Holy Spirit said, "Tell them you are here for the prayer meeting."

"No, I'm not saying that," I responded in my mind.

I knocked.

As the door opened, a small group was gathered in a circle, ready to begin their first weekly prayer meeting. I arrived exactly on time for prayer. The small group of us marveled at what God had just done. This prayer meeting would be our regular, weekly prayer meeting for the next several years.

God had taken me from a catalytic season of change and led me into my new normal, a regular weekly rhythm of prayer and community. The breakthroughs gained during 10 Days would be sustained in regular weekly times of prayer and fellowship.

11

TRANSFORMING REVIVAL IN THE USA (2007-2008)

BACK AT YALE

DURING the summer of 2007, I once again traveled to Yale for the Institute of Campus Revival and Awakening. In 2006, George Otis Jr. had shared amazing stories of transforming revival from the island nation of Fiji. Bodies were healed, the dead were raised, towns were transformed; even the earth and water were healed through the simple power of prayer, fasting, and repentance in this remote nation.

George had shared about the Healing the Land team who were instrumental in this move of God. This year, Savi, the Fijian leader of the Healing the Land team was a keynote speaker. Rhonda Hughey, an American who had been working closely with the native Fijians, shared as well.

Savi and Rhonda were eyewitnesses of what I was longing to see. As they shared their methodology, I was surprised to learn just how similar their strategy was to the vision of 10 Days.

Rhonda and Savi shared how the Healing the Land team operated.

The tribal chief would invite them into a town or village. Often, but not always, this would happen because of an insoluble problem the village was facing. The chief would "stop everything" in the town for seven to ten days. There was a call to fasting along with three daily times of extended prayer. Meanwhile, repentance happened both in the larger meetings and house-to-house, with the Healing the Land team leading villagers to reconcile with neighbors, to repent of sin, and to (literally) get rid of idols. Over and over, the Healing the Land team witnessed a moment when "God came to town," often around seven days into the process. When "God came to town," there would be a sign in the natural world to confirm what was happening spiritually. Most often, the natural sign would be rain. After this, the spiritual atmosphere would shift. Miracles, signs, and wonders would become commonplace, the dead would be raised, and the land would be healed, with miracles affecting soil fertility, the health of the water, and plant and animal life taking place in villages.

My jaw was on the floor. The strategy of the Fijians, stopping everything for a period of seven-to-ten days to pray and repent, was almost identical to what God had shown me for 10 Days. However, if I was right, God wanted to see this exact thing happen all over the world, at the same time, and in an annual, repeatable way. Could it be that 10 Days was God's plan for people around the world to experience the same type of transforming revival that was impacting Fijian villages, but on an annual basis?

I continued to dream with God—what if a Fijian-style transforming revival started touching down in multiple, large cities at the same time? What if western cities had the same experiences with God's power as remote Fijian villages—what if "God came to town" in New York City, or Washington, D.C.?

The Fijians continued to stretch my sense of what was possible, filling my heart with a hunger to see what they were describing happen in the United States. I also realized what we were up against. In a tribal culture, people obey the leader. The chief could shut down a village and lead people into prayer. How could we see that happen in the highly individualistic western nations? How was it possible for cities to shut down for prayer and repentance? At the very least, it would take the engagement of political and business leaders, as well as the church. Most likely, it would take some kind of external crisis as well.

The impossible dreams of God were stirring in my heart.

10 DAYS PENTECOST 2008

In the fall of 2007, Cassi and I did the Ten Days of Awe on our own. For some reason, God didn't lead me to do anything larger. It was becoming clear to me that the fall 10 Days, while a much bigger part of God's plan, was taking longer to mature than the 10 Days Pentecost. While I was eager for the vision to come forth, I also had a new-found patience. He would make everything beautiful in His time. My job was simply to be a steward of the vision He had entrusted me with, and not quit. I continued to watch and wait, trusting Him to do what He showed me in the fullness of time.

In 2008, we headed back to Northfield for a second spring 10 Days. Our event in 2007 completely changed my life. Because of this, I wanted as many of my classmates as possible to have a similar experience. While there were many wonderful things about our seminary experience, the biggest thing missing was a dynamic, face-to-face encounter with the God we spent so much time studying.

I also knew my classmates—no seminary student would ever do 10 Days unless I could make it available for course credit. And so, after hours of work with the administration, we were able to offer 10 Days of Prayer as an elective for course credit at Gordon-Conwell Theological Seminary.

As we began 10 Days 2008, everything was completely different. The incredible experience of John 17 unity that unexpectedly landed the year before was now inexplicably absent. In fact, there were several disagreements. Some people didn't like the worship music; others had theological questions about what was happening.

"The Bible says people should not pray in tongues together without interpretation."

"When that girl sings, she sounds like Jesus is her boyfriend."

"Some of these people are doing weird things—what if it's demonic?"

Many of my seminary friends were struggling with the same issues I had in 2007 and were letting me know about it. But it was more than that. In 2007, it had been difficult for people to think or talk about anything other than the Lord. Somehow, even though we were praying a lot, things still felt, well, rather normal.

Frustrated with our inability to break into a deeper experience of God's presence, we tried a new approach. We invited everyone into three days of fasting, from Sunday night to Wednesday night. We also pulled back on some of our worship led evening sessions and had prayer for three nights that highlighted other kinds of prayer: Scripture, intercession, and silence. On Tuesday night, we had a corporate prayer meeting of about forty people sitting in utter silence for an hour and a half. You could hear empty stomachs gurgling as the minutes ticked slowly by.

LABOR PAINS

On the morning of Wednesday, the seventh day, I was attending to the mundane realities of leading an event, welcoming new families, solving problems, being a host. Our gathering was significantly larger this year. 24/7 prayer was ascending night and day. Good things were happening.

And yet, having tasted John 17 unity in 2007 and realizing we were coming up so short of it, I was restless inside. I needed to get away.

I found a room where I could be alone with God and turned on some worship music, lifting my complaint to the Lord.

"God, if we can't see John 17 unity happen with a group of people who are doing nothing but praying for 10 Days, how will we ever see it happen in the entire church?" I asked.

It wasn't an accusation against God, it was the cry of a desperate heart.

As I cried out to God, I began sobbing and groaning heavily. Waves of tears and groans would come steadily every four to five minutes, last for several minutes, and then lift, and then come again.

A few months earlier, my wife had given birth to our second child, a beautiful little girl named Sabbath. As I was recovering from one of these waves of weeping and groaning in prayer, I had a realization—

"I'm in labor!"

While it struck me as strange for a man to be in labor, no sooner had I realized what was happening than a new wave of weeping and groaning hit me.

After about forty-five minutes, the experience lifted. I felt like a wrung-out sponge. As I found out over the next days, several other people in our group were experiencing labor pains in other parts of the building on the same day.

THE OUTPOURING

Early in the afternoon, on a beautiful spring day, three of us were talking on the yard near the prayer room. Enjoying warm sunshine in a beautiful place with great friends was almost as good as being in worship.

As we continued chatting, we heard a shout from the prayer room. Someone blew a trumpet. Two of us looked at each other—we could both sense it. Something was happening spiritually and we needed to be there right away.

As we entered the room, an outpouring of the Holy Spirit had already begun. We gathered in a circle, holding hands, as the power and presence of God was poured out on us. Several people began spontaneously speaking in tongues for the first time. God was releasing other gifts as well. The presence of God was strong. This was the beginning of what I had prayed for that morning—God was responding.

WHEN GOD COMES TO TOWN

That evening would be unlike anything I had ever experienced. As the worship began, one of the young men, Josiah Armstrong, stood up with a word from the Lord.

Josiah prophesied, "I see a cloud the size of a man's hand."

He was referencing the cloud Elijah's servant saw after Elijah prayed seven times for rain in 1 Kings 18. In the passage, the cloud was the sign that rain was on the way. At that point, we had prayed seven complete days.

He continued, "God is going to send rain in the natural tonight as a sign of what He's doing in the Spirit."

To this day, I don't understand what happened next, but as soon as Josiah said these words, the entire room smelled like rain. As everyone in the room breathed in the scent of rain at the same time, there was a collective, audible gasp.

"What is happening?" I wondered.

I rushed outside to check for rain. All the stars were visible with not a cloud in the sky.

After the outpouring that afternoon and now Josiah's word, we continued late into the night with corporate prayer and worship, followed by ministry to one another in small groups.

Well after midnight, I found myself headed to bed, exhausted but satisfied—what a day! I entered my apartment quietly without turning on any lights, being careful not to wake our children. As I walked in the dark towards my bed, feeling my way forward with my hands, through the open window I heard the sound of a gentle rain just beginning to fall.

And then it hit me—God had come to town.

What the Fijians had described happening over and over in their villages, we were now experiencing right here in the United States. After seven days, God's presence had come flooding in. And just like in Fiji, He had confirmed the spiritual reality of His coming with a natural sign—the rain of Heaven had come.

OVERFLOW

The next three days were wild.

The power of God was evident everywhere and many amazing things were happening. The main thing I remember was the intensity of God's presence. At times, I would be overwhelmed by it. I'd have to retreat to my room and take a nap. When I woke up, I would jump back in the river. I felt like a child on Christmas morning.

Some who had been resistant were now in a different state of mind. Instead of questioning the theological validity of different practices, they had different questions.

"How do you explain what we all witnessed last night?" they asked. "We all just saw a powerful sign. But what does it mean?"

Not sure how to answer, immediately Acts 4 came to mind. In that chapter, the apostles gather for prayer and then an outpouring of the Holy Spirit takes place. The outpouring is accompanied by a physical sign in the natural world—in that case, it was an earthquake that shook the room.

"What we experienced last night is similar to that," I explained. "God did something spiritually and gave us an accompanying sign in the natural world. For the apostles, it was shaking. For us it was rain."

That seemed to make sense to everyone.

NORTHFIELD CALLING

Something else was happening in this outpouring. God was speaking to many of us about what He wanted to do at this incredibly beautiful, entirely empty campus. He was showing us a new vision: He wanted to give Northfield back to His people and make it a center for John 17 unity, a meeting place where the different parts of the church could come together. As we prayed, God revealed vision of a multi-ministry center with a house of prayer, a four year college, local farming, and a training center for missionaries to be sent around the world in the spirit of the Student Volunteers.

God also made it clear to me that our calling to Northfield and New England would be long-term.

We had been praying for God to revive an empty campus for two years. Now, I started to see to God was calling me not only to pray, but also to be part of the answer to my own prayers. Somehow, I was going to be part of this new ministry center at Northfield.

CONCLUSIONS

As in 2007, 10 Days in 2008 was a completely life-changing experience. To this day, the outpouring of 2008 is one of the most powerful encounters with God I have ever had. It was as though God's Kingdom had violently invaded earth—it was almost too much for my human frame to handle.

Through this experience, I learned how each 10 Days experience is different because God is always doing something new. While this one started off more slowly, and I was initially disappointed, it ended up being even more powerful than 10 Days in 2007.

When facing opposition, don't be offended, but love your fellow believers, and trust in God. My friends who initially questioned what was happening later encountered the love and power of God.

I experienced first-hand how 10 Days is a strategy for transforming revival. The kinds of things that were happening in Fiji and around the world were also available in the West. Amazingly, 10 Days was nearly identical to the strategy of the Fijians. While they were leading the way and had far more experience, we had now seen the same thing happen in the USA.

On a personal note, in 2008 it became clear to Cassi and me that God was calling us to Western Massachusetts, Northfield, and New England. Somehow, we were going to be part of the revival of D.L. Moody's legacy. God had poured out His Spirit on us with fresh faith so that somehow the impossible dreams of His heart seemed extraordinarily simple. Nothing is impossible for God.

12

LEARNING HOW TO MOURN (2008-2009)

MOURNING FOR THE LORD'S RETURN

MY visionary experience with the Lord in 2004 was almost entirely about the 10 Days from the Day of Trumpets to the Day of Atonement. And yet, by 2008 we had not yet hosted a public, Ten Days of Awe event. I had learned so much about the rhythm of following the Lord, so I wasn't worried. He takes His time. But I longed to see the fall 10 Days established as God had showed me.

The summer of 2008, starting July 1, I began an intensive season of prayer and fasting to prepare for our first public fall 10 Days at Northfield.

The cry of my heart to the Lord coming into the fast was "show me your glory." It was a cry for personal encounter with God that would overflow into corporate revival. I was still expecting sweeping revival to touch down in the United States at any moment. However, as I followed the Lord into this season of prayer, I found myself overtaken by an intense groaning and longing not for revival and awakening, but for the return of Jesus. I knew what I was experiencing was connected to the "mourning" that would happen among God's people before His return. Just as I had experienced deep prayer and weeping like labor pains for the John 17 unity of the church, now He was giving me a similar experience stretching over days and weeks, this time focused not on unity, but on His second coming.

Jesus Christ is the Son of God, but He is also a real human being destined to return to earth. He's my best friend that I have never met face to face. How could He stay away from us so long? Together as the church, we are called the Bride of Christ. How could we endure separation from our Bridegroom any longer?

The Lord had told me that His people would mourn before His return. I started experiencing what it felt like to mourn *for* His return, to long for His coming with every fiber of my being. As Matthew 9:15 put it, when the Bridegroom is taken away, then they will mourn. I spent that summer learning how to mourn.

A PERSONAL FINANCIAL CRISIS

On the first day of this fast, I was unable to pay a bill on schedule for the first time in my life. As I was beginning this season of mourning for the return of Jesus, God was leading me into the wilderness, a place where I would come to know the Lord's provision as never before. I assumed the wilderness experience would end after forty days. I assumed God would provide, make things right, and I'd be able to pay my bills again. Instead, debts continued to pile up. I was becoming offended with God because of the delay. I was being obedient. I was doing everything He told me to do. He was supposed to provide for me. Instead, I was spiraling into my own personal financial crisis.

BABYLON REFUSES TO MOURN

As we arrived in Northfield and prepared to launch 10 Days on Rosh Hashanah 2008, I received a text from my brother.

"The stock market just lost 777 points."

At the very hour we launched our first, public 10 Days event on the Days of Awe, the entire world was plunging into a financial crisis.

My mind went back to what God had said at the beginning, "Babylon refuses to mourn."

In the context of Revelation 18, we see that judgment on Babylon is connected to God's judgment of an oppressive, global economic system. Somehow, it seemed appropriate that at the very hour we launched what I believed would be a global movement of mourning based on Revelation 18, in that very hour the global economic system, Babylon, was receiving a measure of judgement.

And we, as God's people, in a very small way were coming into mourning.

TEN DAYS OF AWE, 2008

That fall, our 10 Days was a little smaller than the Pentecost events had been, with less people coming and going. It was more of an intercessory assignment than a Holy Ghost blowout. As the 2008 financial crisis took hold, we sensed God calling us to close the gap in prayer and intercede for the people of God, most of whom were not ready to step into a mature, intercessory role. We felt God had positioned us like the 300 Spartans who were ready in advance of the larger Greek army to stave off the enemy's attack. We were ready to fast and pray, and just in time.

God had told me, "My people will mourn before I return," and we were doing our best to mourn together. While I had learned how to do this personally over the summer, I struggled to bring this dynamic from the secret place to a corporate setting. I found this first fall 10 Days to be much less visibly powerful and enjoyable than our other Northfield prayer gatherings. Between the dark theme of mourning and my own personal financial struggles, I battled discouragement the entire time.

Amid this discouragement, the Lord steered me right with a strong word.

In John 5, Jesus highlights four people or things that testify to who He is: John the Baptist, the miraculous signs that He performs, the Father, and the Scriptures. The Lord showed me I had become too dependent on the testimony of miraculous signs, and He wanted to grow me in receiving these other forms of testimony about Jesus—particularly the Father's testimony and the testimony of the Scriptures. I could see clearly that the Lord was right—my personal mood and sense of accomplishment depended too much on what God was doing, and not enough on who He was.

That year, once again we partnered with the New England Alliance in a major regional gathering—this time a Solemn Assembly of repentance right in the middle of the 10 Days. As the Fall 10 Days concluded, we walked away strengthened in our sense of calling to Northfield and assured that we had been in the right place at the right time.

CONCLUSIONS AND QUESTIONS

God had clearly led us to launch the Ten Days of Awe that fall. The timing of our launch, with the advent of the global financial crisis was an undeniable sign. However, it was clear to me that I had a lot to learn.

Foremost in my mind was solving the puzzle of what God meant when He said, "My people will mourn before I return."

I didn't know how to lead people into the mourning God was looking for. I had experienced it personally, but I didn't know how to share it. We had a significant struggle with people mourning as a religious exercise or stepping into intercessory assignments under their own power and not in the grace of God. This heavy, intercessory burden at times led to depression and didn't exhibit the life of the Spirit, which is righteousness, peace, and joy, a life we had experienced so powerfully in the spring 10 Day events.

When I compared the fruit of changed lives, I realized the spring events were more powerful and more visibly productive than the fall 10 Days. I knew I couldn't see everything; I couldn't see how our prayers had moved heaven; yet certainly there must be a way to move heaven and have visible fruit of changed lives as well.

I had questions that needed answering. What did it mean to mourn? And what kind of mourning was God looking for during the 10 Days? How could we mourn as God intended without descending into a heavy, religious spirit?

10 DAYS PENTECOST 2009

In May 2009, I graduated from seminary. Just days later, we were back at Northfield for our fourth 10 Days of Prayer at the Moody property.

I will never fail to marvel at the endless creativity of God. When we seek Him, we find Him. However, we have very little control over how He shows up. In previous 10 Days events, we had experienced John 17 unity and even transforming revival. In 2009, we would experience something completely new: a revival mess.

FRAGRANCE

As we began, there was a strong but very peaceful sense of God's presence. No fireworks through the first forty-eight hours, but something was building under the surface. The presence of prayer and praise filled the building like fragrance—it was gentle, but I could tell the Lord was pleased.

As we approached the first Sunday, I informed everyone we'd have a more relaxed schedule to rest up and prepare for a very full week. Two women had come together, hoping to be touched by God. After almost seventy-two hours in prayer and seeing nothing significant happen, one of the women headed home early. The other decided to stick it out and see what God would do.

That Sunday morning, God took over our meeting and powerfully touched every person, including the woman who stayed. I felt bad for the one who left. She had missed the touch from God she desperately wanted. However, it was a powerful reminder of the necessity and power of perseverance. One never knows what God will do next.

The next day, Monday, the fireworks continued. Many were touched powerfully by the Lord. One man became "stuck" in the same position in the prayer room from the morning session, all the way until well after dinner. He was kneeling, with his eyes closed and hands outstretched, totally frozen for more than seven hours as countless activities swirled around him. He was still as a stone. I had never seen anything like it. When he emerged from the encounter, it was as though a butterfly had come out of the cocoon. He was a new man.

A SINKING SHIP?

There were also ominous signs as we entered the second week. Rough seas threated to turn our gathering into the biggest 10 Days shipwreck since 2005. I had allowed several strangers off the street to come and join the 10 Days for free, and while they used spiritual-sounding language, they seemed to be under a sinister influence. Meanwhile, a young married man was spending inordinate amounts of time with an attractive young woman who was not his wife. How could this be happening at a prayer meeting?

Tuesday night into Wednesday, the sweet fragrance of God's presence had degenerated into tangible demonic oppression that pervaded the atmosphere. Many of the women confessed to being afraid to walk in the hallways at night because of the sense of darkness dominating our prayer meeting. How had things gotten so bad, so fast? The ship was taking on water. I called an emergency meeting with the leadership team, trying to save the event, if it wasn't already too late.

"KEEP MAKING MISTAKES"

On Wednesday night, as we prepared to enter our evening session, we were experiencing tangible demonic oppression. An outside worship team had just arrived to minister and they could feel it. "What's going on here?" they asked. They wanted to leave because things were so bad. I begged them to stay and fight through with us. Things felt, well, evil. Meanwhile, I was calling out to the Lord. As usual, I had no idea what to do.

"Lord, help! What do you want me to do? I don't know what to do. Tell me what to do!" I was desperate.

A strong answer from the Lord resounded in my spirit:

"Keep making mistakes," was all He said.

This struck me as troubling, reassuring, and hilarious all at the same time. I started laughing out loud for no apparent reason. Clearly, I had been making mistakes up to this point. That's how we had gotten into this mess. And the Lord's plan for me was to "keep making mistakes."

"Well, at least that's something I know I can do," I thought.

As the awful, oppressed evening session began, it felt like we were trudging through knee-high mud. Looking back, it's terribly funny just how stuck we were. At the time, it was horrible.

In this moment of suffering, of public and abject leadership failure, the Lord told me to hold on. He showed me a vision of a bus that was about to zip around a hairpin curve at full speed. I knew He was about to take over and change everything in an instant.

My friend Christ Otto (whose first name rhymes with "wrist") was a key part of 10 Days that year. He got up, and publicly rebuked a "spirit of mischief" that was in the room, a phrase he got from John

Wesley. Apparently, Wesley knew something about oppressed revival meetings as well. Then, he had a word of knowledge.

"We are going to take communion now. I want the person or people who are doing drugs to come up right now and repent. Everyone else come and take communion and this atmosphere is going to break," Christ said with a stern voice. A man came forward to the altar, weeping and repenting of drug use.

Everything changed after that, just as the Lord had showed me. In the next twenty-four hours, we kicked out several people who were refusing to repent, including one of my friends who was having an inappropriate relationship with a woman. Somehow, by literally fumbling our way forward, continuing to make mistakes, God was righting the ship.

COME HOLY SPIRIT

The culminating moment was on Friday night. We had a guest minister with us. For some reason, I felt incredibly insecure that evening.

"What if God doesn't show up? I'll look bad." It is a vulnerable place to be when the success or failure of what's happening depends totally on God showing up. The enemy used that righteous vulnerability to attack me. As I worked through these thoughts with the Lord during worship, the presence of God began to come.

Then our guest, Steve Chase, got up. He was sensing God wanted to pour out His Spirit that night. He prayed a simple prayer, something like "Come Holy Spirit." And just like that, the Holy Spirit was poured out on those present. Steve and I, as well as several others, started moving around the room praying for those who were being touched. That night, one of my good friends from seminary, Jordan Easley, was baptized in the Holy Spirit and in joy. Jordan and I had met at Wheaton College in Illinois in 2005 during my first attempt to share the 10 Days vision with the world. Somehow, he and I had reconnected in seminary and he was still doing 10 Days. As he staggered out of the worship room late at night, with a ridiculous grin on his face, I was amazed by the Lord. In spite of all my mistakes, He had done it once again.

Christ Otto asked the Lord why that year had been such a mess. He told him it was because He was training us to operate in the midst of revival. When God moves powerfully, it's often very messy. The Lord wanted us to have some on-the-job training with messy revival.

WE WON'T BE BACK FOR A LONG TIME

As we concluded 10 Days 2009 with the Global Day of Prayer, Christ came up to me, crying. I was tired and happy that we had ended well. The tears just didn't make sense.

"What's wrong?" I asked.

"The Lord says we will not be back at Northfield for a long time."

"What do you mean?" I asked. "We have a contract for the fall."

"Well, that's what the Lord says." Christ had a way of hearing from the Lord that was often very accurate.

I didn't know what to do in response to this word. We had done four 10 Days of Prayer events at Northfield. God had led us there supernaturally, and I liked doing them. Naively, I imagined we'd keep doing them indefinitely, leading somehow into God's plan and purpose for us to be active in ministry on the campus in the future. However, that was not to be the case.

FALL 10 DAYS 2009

I didn't know what to do in response to Christ's word. If we pulled out of our contract for the fall, it would just be a self-fulfilling prophecy. So, I decided to keep our plans steady and leave the result up to the

Lord. God was increasingly showing me how to respond to what He was saying with faith and wisdom.

Sure enough, several weeks before our fall 10 Days in 2009 was to take place, our contacts at Northfield-Mt. Hermon called and informed us they were canceling our fall event. We could not go back to Northfield. With just a few weeks before the Days of Awe, this put us in an awkward position.

Thankfully, the Lord prepared a place for us. We were planning another New England Solemn Assembly at Raffoul Najem's church in Lowell. Pastor Raffoul graciously agreed to host our 10 Days at his facility.

WHAT DOES IT MEAN TO MOURN?

In 2004, God had showed me to "call His people to mourn" during the Ten Days of Awe. After five years, I had no idea how to do this without everyone leaving depressed.

We had tried the strategy of confessing every sin, corporate and personal. We had tried our best to mourn what was wrong in the world. We had even tried to "mourn for the Return of Jesus." But it had not led to the same type of fruit as our spring 10 Day gatherings where we simply let the Holy Spirit move freely. When we attempted to mourn, it just felt like a bad prayer meeting.

What did God mean when He said "My people will mourn before I return"? What did it look like, feel like, sound like for a group of people to enter that type of mourning, together?

Up to this point, we had been doing it wrong. At the very least, we were in the very early stages of learning, like a baby learning to walk who mostly has falling on his resume. What would it mean to really get it, to enter into the kind of mourning about which God says "Blessed are those who mourn, for they will be comforted"? How could we mourn in a way that released the blessing of God?

SEARCHING THE SCRIPTURES

As I strove to understand what God wanted, I dove into the Scriptures, seeking insight into this concept.

I began to clearly see that "mourning" is a heart-felt response to something we lack or have lost. Mourning is how the heart responds when something or someone valuable is missing. This opened my mind to the connection between mourning and prayer.

Paradoxically, it's mourning, the recognition of what we lack, that opens the door for us to receive what we are lacking from God. If we wrongly think that we can see and yet we are blind and we will not ask God for sight. But if we acknowledge our blindness, and ask God for sight, He will open our eyes.

In the Kingdom, recognizing what we lack and have lost is the key to receiving and recovering it. If we don't realize what we are missing, we will never pray; we will never ask God to supply it. Now, it was beginning to make sense why God wanted His people to mourn before the return of Jesus. He wants us to experience the absence of His Son, so that we will ask Him to send Jesus. He's asking us to "mourn" so He can answer our prayers. But if we are satisfied with things as they are, we will not ask, we will not seek, and we will not knock.

As I meditated on this principle, I found myself repeating a bad Scriptural pun over and over, because it gets at the ultimate truth: "Joy comes in the Mourning." It was really true—God wanted us to mourn so that He could release joy! And He wanted His whole church to mourn for 10 entire days, stopping everything else, because He wanted to release an outpouring of joy on His people—first through an unprecedented outpouring of the Holy Spirit, and then through the return of His Son to rule and reign.

Godly mourning has different aspects.

It starts with us *personally* recognizing how much of God we lack in our lives. This is just as true for the seasoned saint as it is for the new believer. Because there is so much of God to receive, all of us are in the very worst spiritual poverty. Compared to the lowliest saint in heaven, all of us on earth are living in a cardboard box. We need to recognize our lack so we can receive *more* of God. If we are not aware of our poverty, we won't ask. If we don't ask, we won't receive.

As we are touched personally, our hearts begin aligning with God's heart. Now, we are not only aware of what we lack personally, but as friends of God, what He lacks begins to touch our heart. This recognition leads us into intercessory mourning for the unfulfilled plans and desires of God's heart.

God has clearly stated many of His plans and heart's desires in Scripture. Incredibly, He has chosen to partner with us in prayer and mission to fulfill these promises. As I poured over the Scriptures, four major, unfulfilled promises leapt out at me. These four major promises seemed to have a fulfillment before Jesus returned, but they had not been fulfilled yet. They also served as summary statements for other future promises.

The Scriptures declare God's plan and heart's desire for:

The gospel of the Kingdom to be preached to all nations (Matthew 24:14).

A massive outpouring of the Holy Spirit before the return of the Lord (Joel 2:28).

The supernatural unity of the church, "as the Father and Son are one" (John 17:20-23, Ephesians 4:13).

The salvation of the Jewish people (Romans 11).

These four Biblical promises seemed to summarize all that we were asking God to do in the earth.

Beyond our personal spiritual poverty, and the tarrying of God's promises, most importantly, we mourn because Jesus is absent.

The Father was looking for a fulfillment of Matthew 9:15, "The friends of the bridegroom cannot mourn while the bridegroom is with them, but a day is coming when the bridegroom will be taken away, and then they will fast." God wants us to mourn and fast in an extraordinary way because His Son is absent.

The fall 10 Days was ultimately a time to say to the Lord Jesus, "We are not okay that you are not here."

As I came to understand it, the mourning God was looking for could be summed up in three prayers.

Lord, I see I am in spiritual poverty. I turn away from known sin. Show me my hidden faults and fill me with your Spirit.

Lord, I see that your priorities and promises are still unfulfilled after almost 2,000 years. Pour out your Spirit and unite your church. May the gospel message go to every nation and be received by the Jewish people as well.

Lord, I am heartbroken by the absence of your Son, our Messiah. May your Kingdom come on earth as it is in Heaven. Come Lord Jesus.

UNDERSTANDING JOY

At the same time I was coming into this understanding of mourning, I was exposed to an extreme charismatic stream in the church with a heavy emphasis on experiencing the joy of the Lord. These folks taught that because of the finished work of the cross, there was no place for any sorrow or mourning in the believer's life. All we had to do was believe and receive His joy. I could tell some of these folks were off, just as I had been in 2005—they could have used a review of Edwards's "Errors and Excesses"; however, they were certainly carrying something, and it was contagious.

Their focus on joy and rejection of mourning made me question everything I was doing.

"Am I completely wrong about God wanting us to mourn?" I asked Cassi. "Is this entire calling just a figment of my religious imagination?"

Cassi encouraged me to stay the course with what God had called me to do and not get off-track because of someone else's teaching. We all see in part, and we need one another.

Regardless of any errors and excesses, there was an impartation of the joy of the Lord that took place.

FALL 10 DAYS 2009

During the fall 10 Days that year, even as we emphasized mourning, we experienced the same power and presence of God we had seen during the spring 10 Days. The church where we met had a school, and although they were not even in earshot of us, the school and the teachers reported a profound peace among the students during the days we were present.

We divided our three daily prayer sessions according to these different kinds of mourning.

The morning sessions were for "personal repentance" or mourning before the Lord on behalf of ourselves. Rather than striving to be spiritual, beating ourselves up, and confessing every sin we had committed since childhood, we simply waited on God in worship, opening up our hearts to Him like a book. This was our personal mourning, simply acknowledging our spiritual poverty, asking the Lord to reveal hidden faults, and resting in His presence. Rather than being heavy and discouraging as before, these times of mourning were refreshing and encouraging and led to genuine, 180-degree repentance.

In the afternoons, we interceded according to the four major unfulfilled promises in the New Covenant, crying out for the gospel to go to all nations, for unity in the church, for the Holy Spirit to be poured out, and for the Jewish people to acknowledge their Messiah. These times of prayer were powerful, enjoyable, and effective.

Finally, in the evenings, we would try to enter into a longing for the Lord's return. And while it didn't feel like we knew how to do it in a corporate context, it was clear God was pleased with our efforts. He kept showing up and meeting us as we sought His face.

As the fall 10 Days ended that year, I knew we had finally hit the mark. Maybe we were toddlers just starting to walk, but we were taking steps with both feet, maybe even running a little bit. We had finally done something like what the Lord had in mind when He said, "My people will mourn before I return." It was encouraging, edifying, and just plain beautiful to behold. It was weaker and smaller than He wanted, but it was right. It was His people, waiting on Him, humbling themselves, reckoning with their need, agreeing with Him in prayer for His plans and purposes, and longing for Jesus to return. This was what the Lord was after during 10 Days.

As we concluded our final prayer gathering, it happened. I was exhausted, completely poured out, and really looking forward to our big meal once the fast ended; not in the most spiritual of mindsets.

As soon as we prayed the last prayer, and said "Amen," the Holy Spirit dropped on me and the person next to me. I was overwhelmed with joy—drunk in the Spirit as we sometimes say, full of the love and joy of God. As I had been saying over and over that year, "Joy comes in the mourning!" And now it had happened: God had poured out joy on those who mourn.

EPILOGUE TO FIVE EARLY RETREATS

I've shared detailed accounts of all five 10 Day retreats from 2007 to 2009, because of their foundational role in the formation of the movement. There's hardly a day that goes by where I don't remember and draw from lessons learned in this incredible school of the Holy Spirit.

This chapter would be incomplete without sharing one more significant answer to prayer.

This entire season centered around the beautiful Northfield campus, founded by evangelist D.L. Moody. The massive property, comprising hundreds of acres and dozens of large buildings, had been for sale since 2005, and was originally listed at forty million dollars.

Ever since we arrived, and unknowingly reprised Moody's 1880 ten day prayer meeting, we had asked God to bring a Christian buyer for the campus who would bring it back in line with its original purpose. We wanted to see spiritual renewal, John 17 unity, and a 24/7 house of prayer on that property so that a new Student Volunteer Movement would come forth once again. We also asked God to do it for cheap.

At some point, several praying women had buried a glass jar on the campus with the number $10 million written on it. It was an acted-out prayer, a prophetic act, asking the Lord to give the campus to believers for one-quarter of the asking price.

It turned out that our inability to return to Northfield in the fall of 2009 was connected to the fact that the campus was in the final stages of a sale. The Green Family, who were believers and the owners of Hobby Lobby, would purchase the campus for the astonishing price of $100,000.

As Ephesians 3:20 says, "to Him who is able to do far more abundantly beyond what we can ask or think according to the power that works in us…"

God had done far more than any of us could ask or think. He had brought the campus back into the family for 100 times *less* than the low price we had asked for and imagined. God had heard our prayers and gone beyond. While we could claim no credit for what happened, we couldn't help but see that God was answering our prayers.

13

CITY-WIDE (2009-2010)

AN initial answer to our prayers at Northfield had come in spectacular fashion. Ironically, it resulted in us no longer being able to do events there.

This disruption, forced on us by external events, led me back to the original experience with the Lord.

The original vision was a city.

Everything in the city stopped for days on end as exalting Jesus became the preeminent focus of every heart.

The original vision was a city that looked like the throne room in Heaven.

I had now seen what was possible when groups of people stop everything for prayer. We had experienced Heaven touching Earth. If we could somehow find a way to scale our Northfield experiences up to a city-wide level, it could turn the world upside down.

God was kicking us out of the familiarity of the nest, out of the incubator of the Northfield retreats, and into a city-wide context. Ready or not, it was time for 10 Days to fly.

WHERE WOULD GOD SEND THE LETTER?

I was already a member of a strong pastoral group on the North Shore of Boston in the Beverly/Salem area. In the fall of 2009, I began meeting with the pastors one by one. I asked a simple question: "If Jesus wanted to send a letter to the church in our city, what would the address be?"

Clearly, the address wasn't Christ the Redeemer, The Harbor, or Second Baptist. As we all realized, the New Testament was written to "city" churches, to the churches of Ephesus, Laodicea, and Corinth. And yet, our historic divisions left us with very little sense of a city-wide church. We certainly didn't have a common address.

While it was clear that we had inherited historic divisions, much of what had caused those divisions was no longer dividing the people in our group. We had some small theological distinctives, but for the most part we believed the Bible, loved Jesus, and liked C.S. Lewis and Billy Graham. More than that, we really enjoyed being together. Our churches were almost divided by force of habit. We began to dream together about what the church in a city would look like if we moved and functioned as one body.

Clearly, unity didn't mean merging all the congregations together. The value of smaller congregations was immediately evident. The New Testament talked about that as well—there was a city-wide church, with city-wide elders. And yet, there were smaller home churches where most church life happened. These home churches were like our congregations, and the elders of the city were like our pastors' group.

Just as it was important for local churches to meet weekly, it also seemed important for the city-wide church to come together from time to time. If the local church met once or twice a week, would it make sense for the city-wide church to come together once or twice a year?

And, as it happened, I knew of a strategy designed to unite city-wide churches in prayer on an annual basis. I was starting to see the potential of 10 Days to help city-wide churches rediscover their corporate identity and walk together in unity.

A CITY-WIDE BLUEPRINT

Seeing the end goal of the vision and knowing how to get there are two completely different things. God wanted cities stop to everything and honor His Son. But what did that look like, exactly?

This was no longer theoretical. Like an architect designing a home, we now had to map out what 10 Days would look with specific details, so that dozens of leaders and hundreds of people who would never meet in person could all understand the part they were to play. We needed city-wide blueprints.

As three of us from the pastors' group discussed and dreamed at a local café, the idea dawned on us.

10 Days had…well, ten days. What if ten different churches each hosted one night? They could lead a two-hour prayer and worship gathering. As a way of deepening our unity, we could take communion together in each church that was willing to open the table. Each congregation could host in their own location, their own unique style, and organize and lead the evening they were hosting. Inviting each congregation to take leadership of part of 10 Days would honor the unique gifts of each house. Honoring one another above ourselves was one of the keys to unity, so this was essential.

The vision for nightly meetings was exciting, but at Northfield it was abiding in God's presence over long periods of time that had the greatest impact. How could we incorporate that reality into a city-wide context?

We decided we would host prayer throughout the day in partnership with a local house of prayer. This would remain in one location while the evening gatherings marched around the city from place to place.

We sketched our ideas out on a yellow legal pad. A city-wide blueprint for 10 Days was beginning to take shape.

The idea seemed incredibly easy to implement, much simpler organizationally than our 10 Day retreats. We pitched the idea at our next pastors' gathering and then followed up with several one-on-one meetings. After a few weeks, the schedule was full. Ten local churches hosted ten nights of prayer, worship, and communion leading up to Pentecost Sunday and the Global Day of Prayer. We also hosted prayer from seven a.m. to five p.m. daily at a local house of prayer right in the heart of the city.

Almost six years after receiving the vision, it finally happened. The church of the Beverly/Salem Massachusetts region prayed together for 10 Days. 10 Days had now happened at a city-wide level.

GROWING THE CITY-WIDE CHURCH

In the wake of this season of prayer, there was a notable increase in the unity of the Spirit in our local pastors' group. It was clear that love, trust, friendship, and fellowship were increasing. It's hard to explain what changed, but 10 Days had somehow drawn us closer together than ever before. We began dreaming how we could functionally pastor the city together. I was starting to see firsthand the power of 10 Days to bring city-wide churches out of historic division and back to the model clearly laid out in Scripture.

Our first city-wide event was also much larger than the retreats. As had happened at the retreats, in addition to answered prayer, lives were visibly transformed by the power and presence of God. People were saved, believers were encouraged, new callings were discovered, new gifts poured out. On a personal level, it was incredible to see more and more people touched by a vision God had entrusted to me.

Doing 10 Days in a city was a massive step forward. I was so thankful to the Lord.

As I always did after each 10 Days, I compared what happened to the original vision and to previous years.

While God moved powerfully, I couldn't help but notice the depth of what God was doing was less than we had experienced multiple times in the early retreats.

I thought I understood why: at the retreats, most of the participants had set the entire time apart to be with the Lord. The act of consecration, stopping everything, seemed to be key to God moving in greater power. In contrast, at our first city-wide event, most participants kept working and going about their lives, and then came to a handful of evening prayer meetings. While this was still having an impact, I knew there was so much more available. I was longing to see the experiences of Northfield duplicated at a city level.

Also, after successfully modeling 10 Days in a smaller city, I felt the Lord leading me to Boston, the hub of the New England region. I believed God wanted to see large cities around the globe experience the same kind of transforming revival that had hit tiny Fijian villages. We needed to model 10 Days in a major city. It was clear to me: Boston was the next step.

In the spring and summer of 2010, I began taking steps to see a fall 10 Days in Boston.

Surprisingly, the Lord pressed pause on the endeavor. At the time, God had led me to serve and support a number of major projects initiated by other people. He wanted me to lay aside my personal calling from Him for a time in order to serve and help others.

"Let 10 Days die and go into the ground this fall." He told me.

I was excited—I knew that this was God's strategy for multiplication. And yet, it was incredibly hard to do. I knew God wanted to see cities around the world praying in one accord. And yet, after six long years, all I had to show was a handful of successful gatherings. We had so far to go. How could God be asking us to lay it down?

Six years after receiving the vision, we were right back where we started. Cassi and I doing the fall 10 Days on our own at home.

How would this vision ever come to pass?

14

10 DAYS BOSTON (2010-2011)

AS winter 2010 approached, I began hearing from the Lord quite clearly.

"Pray for snow."

This seemed like an odd prayer, but it also seemed fun. Who doesn't like a good snow day?

I prayed and figured God would answer me quickly, so I was disappointed the next day when it didn't snow. But I persevered through late November and into early December, well past the point when we would normally receive our first snow. Driving back from a ministry meeting in Boston, riding in the passenger seat, I was having a conversation with the Lord about it.

"Did you really say to pray for snow?" I asked. It didn't seem very important and obviously my prayers were not working.

No sooner had I asked God this question, than a truck with a New Hampshire license plate drove by. The vanity plate read "PRY4SNO."

I don't always know what to make of unusual coincidences like this, but they seem to happen more often when we are walking with God. I took it as an answer to prayer: Keep praying for snow.

And so, my prayer times became very snow-centric.

In the last prayer set at our house of prayer before Christmas, I found myself singing a spontaneous song, "Let it Snow" to the tune of "Let it Rain." Afterwards, I turned around and looked out the window. The first flurries of the year were starting to fall. The other men who were praying with me said "I thought you were praying that because you saw the snow—you started just as soon as the first flakes appeared." I had no idea. I always prayed for snow. And yet, this snowfall amounted to nothing, just a few flakes.

"What is this all about?" I asked the Lord. And I kept praying for snow. And yet, for all the prayer, it was not a white Christmas.

SNOWMAGGEDON

The day after Christmas, the first storm hit. And after that for over a month, every five to seven days we were hit by massive blizzards. From the end of December, through January and early February we were buried under the biggest blanket of snow I had ever seen. Each week we would get twelve, eighteen, or twenty-four inches; sometimes more than two feet per snowstorm. News outlets started calling it "Snowmageddon."

Personally, I had gone from skeptical about praying for snow to surprised, and from surprised to amazed. I shared this unusual testimony with others, who were often less than appreciative. The volume of snow was creating significant hardship and disruption. Our landlord came over to move snow off the roof so it wouldn't collapse under the weight. He had lived in that region his whole life, so I asked if this kind of snow was normal. The "blizzard of '78" was his closest comparison; a snowstorm in 1978 so famous I had heard about it even though it happened before I was born. So no, even for our snow-loving region, this was not normal.

Every time I shared the testimony of answered prayer, it seemed a new storm with twelve to twenty-four inches would arrive. My lamp-post, which was about ten feet high, was barely visible. Our lawn furniture was a distant memory. In early February, we got one of the biggest storms of the season. And after this storm, the Lord told me, "Stop telling the testimony."

I had no idea why—did I do something wrong? Was I bragging about my prayers being answered? However, after I stopped telling the testimony, we had no more major storms the rest of the year. I guess God had made his point to me and wanted to have mercy on the region—to say we were sick of snow would be a massive understatement.

INTERPRETATION

Although this is not part of the 10 Days story proper, I share this as an encouragement regarding our prayers for the pouring out of God's Spirit on the earth. Initially, I was thinking short term and small. God wanted me to think longer term and bigger; it was not just to be one outpouring, but multiple, massive, and successive revivals, so much so that people would be "sick of it." The connection between stopping the testimony and the snowfall stopping is also interesting. It highlights how declaring the works of God seems to cause Him to do even more. When it was time to turn the snow off, He just said "stop telling the testimony."

God has a pre-established plan that He wants to work out in partnership with His people—He invites us to pray with perseverance, not losing heart. When it's time for the snow to begin, it will begin. When it's time for it to stop, when God says "enough," He will tell us to stop sharing the testimony, and it will stop.

I think it was not a coincidence that God gave this sign just as we were about to start a new season of 10 Days, a season that in a few years would spark thousands of extended prayer gatherings all over the world, oddly seeming to thrive best in the hardest and darkest places. God's message is clear. Pray, don't stop praying, keep praying, and know that He will send "swift justice" in response to our faithful prayers.

Finally, I want to highlight the encouragement of this type of sign. This season was one of intense trial, testing, and difficulty for me. To see such a tangible answer to prayer literally surrounding us was a great encouragement. Every time I looked outside that winter, I remembered God heard my prayers.

MORE STRANGE WEATHER

On the evening of February 15, 2011, we had dinner at my friend Kelly Steinhaus's apartment to discuss moving forward with 10 Days Boston in the fall of 2011. The weather that day was very strange, an unseasonably warm seventy-five degrees. Contrasting this warmth were piles of snow on the sidewalk higher than our heads. We walked through snow tunnels in T-Shirts, enjoying a summer day in the middle of the snowiest winter any of us had ever seen.

As we gathered that night with about fifteen people to worship, there was a clear sense of God's presence. As we prayed and asked God if we should move forward, it thundered. Thunder in winter is incredibly rare and I know many of us took it as confirmation from the Lord. I didn't understand it all but I knew after that night, we were going to do 10 Days in Boston that year.

PIVOT TO THE FALL 10 DAYS

From my initial vision, I knew the fall 10 Days was the focal point of what God had called me to do. However, up to that point, the 10 Days Pentecost had been bigger and better. The Days of Awe had always been smaller and almost experimental.

The momentum of the last seven years led me to believe we would do 10 Days Boston in the spring. Why not lead with our strength? As we talked, Kelly saw it differently:

"I think we need to do 10 Days during the fall this year."

Something in her simple declaration made me realize we were at a pivot point. While the fall 10 Days had taken longer to develop, now it was time for it to come into greater prominence. We were just getting into the part of the story where this major thing that God wanted to do would begin to happen. I'm so thankful my ministry partner had the sensitivity to see what I couldn't.

PLANNING 10 DAYS BOSTON

Kelly, Frank Mwebesa (an African prayer leader), and I formed the core planning team for 10 Days Boston. Kelly, like me, had a strong calling towards John 17 unity that she was just starting to walk in. I was excited to work with someone with a similar calling. Frank was doing regular, monthly prayer gatherings throughout the Boston region, focusing especially on engaging African immigrant churches.

Through the spring, we met monthly. All we would do in our planning meetings was worship, pray, and listen to the Lord. What an easy and enjoyable planning strategy!

BLUEPRINTS AND A MASTER PLAN

As we ministered to the Lord, He began to give us new insights into how to bring a city together for prayer.

God showed us an image of a "sleeping giant" tied down by thousands of little ropes, like Gulliver among the Lilliputians. Individually, the ropes and bonds were insufficient to hold down the giant, but together they kept him immobilized. We saw that they were all small things—minor offenses, sins, and unresolved interpersonal problems preventing the church from being who God had made her to be. And yet, these small snares of the enemy were holding down the giant.

In the vision, we saw that the giant had a "black" arm and a "white" arm. When both arms moved together, the giant was able to escape from its bondage. We felt God was saying that the black church and the white church working together would be key to seeing this sleeping giant arise in Boston. As a practical way of walking out this vision, we would end up splitting daytime prayer between two ministries known for prayer, one predominantly white, and one mostly black.

As we faced the reality of working in a large city, it was clear that three of us could not unite the church in Boston on our own. Instead, we would need to find other leaders in the city with gifts to unite their communities.

Building off the model of 10 Days on the North Shore, we now looked for ten co-conveners to lead each night—pastors or leaders who would invite multiple ministries to worship and pray together. As it turned out, some evening gatherings would be effectively led by twelve or more congregations working together. At the end of the process, we would have over fifty congregations leading 10 Days Boston.

WAITING ON GOD AND THE POWER OF INVITATION

This developed a process that I now call "master-planning." Kelly, Frank, and I waited on God, then mapped out a plan of the entire 10 Days in response to what we heard from Him. With this sense of priorities, we would then make phone calls and fill in the schedule. While not every call or idea worked, the final schedule was about 80% of what we worked out in times of prayer. At the end of the day, organizing 10 Days in a large city could be as simple as making ten to twenty phone calls.

WHY CAN'T WE WORK ON THIS SOONER?

After waiting on God in the spring and clearly seeing the path forward, we felt no release from the Lord to plan the event. I organized a powerful spring 10 Days on the North Shore. May passed, then June, then July came. Suddenly, we were just over two months from the beginning of 10 Days and we had done nothing aside from listening to God and mapping out what it would look like.

While some of you may have the impression that I'm not a planner because so much of this book has been about last-minute miracles, that's not the case. My preference, especially with complex events like this, is to have ample time to plan and arrange, and then to plan in space for freedom and spontaneity. As we met just after the fourth of July, we were at a decision point.

Kelly was direct. "Are we doing this or what?"

"Let's pray and ask God," I replied. At this point, I had no idea what God was doing.

As we prayed, the answer was a clear "yes" from the Lord. We could now begin organizing, building a website, setting up a schedule, and creating promotional materials. However, something continued to bother me.

"Lord, why wouldn't you let us start working on this earlier?" I asked. When God's ways are confusing to us, an honest question goes a long way.

In my spirit, I heard the Lord say, "Because I want to give you grace to do it quickly."

I found that answer satisfying—getting more done in less time appealed to my American sense of efficiency. Now that we've seen hundreds of unique 10 Days events organized, I have a different perspective on that word. Because we had pulled together a complex event in a major city quickly, it's provided a basis to encourage others that God can do the same thing for them. Since then, we've seen people pull larger 10 Day gatherings together with even less lead time. Sometimes, God wants us to wait. Other times, He wants us to move quickly. It's about His grace and His voice, not our organizational abilities.

OBJECTIONS TO THE TEN DAYS OF AWE

As we prepared to do the Fall 10 Days for the first time in a city-wide context, there were some interesting objections both from within the team and from those we were trying to invite to this city-wide prayer meeting.

This is Impossible

I think this type of objection is common to any undertaking that people haven't seen before. There are many reasons people say this—some good (trying to save you from doing something foolish), some bad (actively trying to discourage you from following Jesus), some just human (they're disappointed with God, and it has limited their ability to hope and dream, or your vision just doesn't connect to their assignment).

The problem was, doing 10 Days in Boston often seemed impossible to me as well.

I combatted these doubts by building up my faith through worship, clearly hearing God's direction, and the encouragement of like-minded brothers and sisters. A small group of friends, in agreement, can take on the world.

Offense

Because other believers can be unintentional "ministers of discouragement" it is essential to keep short accounts and to forgive and love those who are opposing you. They're not your enemies; they're just not seeing what you see yet. In this season, discouragement came from close friends who genuinely loved me and from people I didn't know well but admired. The key here was not receiving the wound of discouragement *and* continuing to love the friend or brother in the Lord.

I've observed many people start in a John 17 type ministry, often with a real sense of calling. Most people I've witnessed personally in this type of ministry do not make it a full year, just as I didn't make it a full year after receiving the 10 Days vision. One of the major causes of drop out is offense at other believers.

<u>Indifference</u>

Indifference is the passive version of "this is impossible." While we were passionate to see the Body of Christ united in prayer, many people, even those we thought would be excited about seeing the city pray together, were completely indifferent.

Once again, we learned to offer what we were doing freely, with no expectation that people would say "yes." We learned to think the best of others who decided not to participate.

Also, we learned to accept our role: We were inviting people to do something, but they did not answer to us and owed us nothing. By offering this freedom to our fellow believers, we avoided the trap of offense that plagued me in 2005. I'll say it again: offer others a free opportunity to encounter God in a life-changing way and think the best of them when they turn you down.

<u>Why are we doing these Jewish Feasts?</u>

One objection I heard often in the early days was related to celebrating the Jewish feast days. To point out the obvious, praying from the Day of Trumpets to the Day of Atonement has not been common throughout church history. I didn't grow up doing these feasts. Neither did the vast majority of believers I connected with. It seemed strange to many that we would observe these festivals.

The strategy the Lord gave me in 2011 was to place the emphasis firmly on Jesus's prayer in John 17. Our materials shared that 10 Days was based on these feasts, but that wasn't our main point. Jesus wants us to be one, and we are gathering to pray for that and for God to move in our city. When people asked, I would point out that the feasts were part of our common biblical heritage. Even though historically we had not observed them, there was no biblical reason we couldn't. I also cultivated a message of freedom regarding the feasts—Colossians 2 teaches us we are free to observe feasts, days, seasons…and also free not to. Jesus Himself is the fulfillment of these feasts, so above all, we needed to keep the focus on Him. We avoided any kind of teaching that the church was required to observe these times or that we'd been sinning for 2,000 years by not observing them.

By listening to the Lord and keeping the focus right, after people experienced the moving of God during 10 Days, often there was an increased interest in the fall feasts.

Once again, contra 2005 where we tried to get everything all at once, we took a long-term view—our goal was not to see everything happen in one year but to take the next step and trust God to bring the fullness at just the right time.

Can we ditch the mourning?

One of the strongest objections to 10 Days was around the idea of "mourning." "Why can't we ditch the idea of mourning and just focus on unity? After all, people have enough sorrow and sadness in their lives. Jesus gives us the oil of joy instead of mourning." I heard these objections often even from good friends, people who would gladly take a bullet for me.

At times, I just threw up my hands hearing this. I hadn't asked to be the "mourning guy." I didn't always love my calling, it wasn't my idea;

but I had to be faithful to what God had given me. Even if we didn't understand why it was important, or didn't like it, we could trust that God would show us and make it beautiful in its time.

Around this time, I began calling 10 Days "the ugly duckling." It was too long, too big, too demanding of time and effort, based on the wrong feasts, and focused on mourning—no one wants to fast and mourn—so how would we see it spread through an entire city? Every single element of this vision was undesirable and unattractive, seemingly designed to push as many people away as possible.

Could it be that like the ugly duckling, 10 Days would one day become beautiful? That was my hope.

THE PLANNING PROCESS

By stepping out in faith, persevering in love, and refusing the temptation of offense, 10 Days Boston was starting to come together.

About eight of our "master planned" hosts said yes, and we easily filled in the rest.

We mostly organized gatherings around neighborhoods: Jamaica Plains, Cambridge, Downtown, Mattapan, Brighton, Lexington. By inviting Kingdom-minded conveners to gather people, we easily surpassed fifty congregations involved in leading 10 Days Boston.

We also organized gatherings around language and culture: we had Haitian churches and African immigrant congregations; we even had a night where Messianic Jews and Arabs hosted together. By working with friends like Brian Corcoran, Gregg Detwiler, and Dana Baker, who had been fostering cross-cultural partnerships in the city for years, we were able to quickly establish lines of trust based on their years of service in Boston. Also, the fact that we just wanted to see the city united in prayer helped—that seemed to be something everyone could get behind.

The Lord was giving us grace to do it quickly, and we marveled at how everything was coming together. However, while all these incredible things were happening, I was undergoing a uniquely difficult and painful personal trial.

INTO THE PROMISES, UNDER DURESS

That summer, the Lord gave me a vision:

He showed me a fishing bobber, ducking under water in massive waves and then popping up again. He was laughing, and said to me, "You're a bobber—no matter how many waves submerge you, you keep popping up." The Lord seemed more amused by this nickname than I was—I was the one being buffeted by all the waves.

Then, he showed me a river roaring in all its strength. I knew it was the Jordan River. I was excited.

"You're about to cross the Jordan River, but it's going to feel like you're crossing the Red Sea," He told me.

Unfortunately, I knew exactly what that meant. I was about to enter the "promised land"—the realm of things God had promised me—but the transition into that season was going to be under duress. Just as Israel crossed the Red Sea while pursued by the massive Egyptian army, leading to utter despair and panic on their side, similarly, I'd be entering into the promises under duress. My excitement turned to steely resolve mixed with dread. Pain was coming, but by God's grace, we would get through it and it would be worth it.

The summer of 2011 was the culminating moment of an extended season of financial difficulty. Suddenly, we had to move. The daughter of our landlord, who had a family of seven, was moving into our home, coming back in a hurry after some difficult experiences on the mission field, and we needed to move out by August 1.

We were three months behind on rent and had no money to move into a new place. Not only that, the finances for basic necessities were tighter than ever. Many days during this season we pillaged the change jars, wanting to make sure that we were using everything God had given us.

In the middle of this we were seeing incredible financial miracles, the kinds of things George Mueller and other mission pioneers had experienced. We knew God was with us and providing for us, but for some reason He allowed things to be incredibly tight at that time.

We blew through our August move-out deadline, still unable to pay our back rent, much less pay for a new home. The other family with five kids moved into the house while we were still there with our four kids. They had to be there and we had to leave, but we had nowhere to go. While the other family was incredibly gracious, with nine small kids total in the house, we needed to leave, and fast.

Finally, by the middle of September, six weeks after our initial deadline to move, God provided the funds for the back rent and then first month's rent in a new home. Needing to move my family in just a few days, we could not find a long-term rental. He opened a beautiful door for us on an exclusive, private beach for a "winter rental," the same way we had entered Massachusetts. God had come through and made a way through the violent waters. We were thankful to Him, but the pressure of the circumstance was one of the more challenging moments in our journey.

At the end of the day, it was just what the Lord said: "A Jordan River crossing that felt like the Red Sea."

PROMISED LAND

And 10 Days Boston was, without a doubt, the beginning of the "promised land" God had shown me in 2004. While it was not the fullness of the 10 Days vision, we did see over fifty churches in one of the most post-Christian cities in America unite in fasting, prayer, worship, and repentance.

Each night was special. Our first gathering was hosted by five different Korean churches. While I did not understand a word of what was spoken, my Spirit was on fire as we prayed and worshipped together. It was amazing how the Holy Spirit could transcend language and culture to unite hearts.

On the third night, we met together in Cambridge with Bishop Brian Greene and thirteen different Cambridge congregations. Bishop Greene and I had prayed together at a pastors' prayer summit in Boston. That brief time of prayer together had knit our hearts, and this partnership was a direct outflow of the prayer summit. The sanctuary was packed out as God visited us powerfully.

At one point in the evening, Kelly asked me, "I've never been in revival, but this is what it feels like, right?"

"Yes," I said. "This is revival. This is what revival feels like."

As I recognized from my experiences at Northfield, it was also what John 17 unity felt like. Now it was happening just down the street from Harvard and MIT. God was moving so powerfully, one of the pastors described arriving late as "riding in on a wave of the Spirit that started well outside the church." The local leaders remarked on "what God was beginning that night for Cambridge" while other leaders remarked how this was simply another level of unity, building on what God had done. It was a memorable visitation of the Holy Spirit to the city-wide church of Cambridge.

BEYOND RACIAL RECONCILIATION

The daytime prayer sessions were my favorite part. There was nothing better than lingering for long hours with the Lord. During the smaller, daytime prayer gatherings we saw a powerful fulfillment of the vision of the "white arm and black arm" working together to free the sleeping giant.

During the last few days there was a movement of racial reconciliation unlike anything I had ever seen. While there were moments of repentance, it was primarily something new that God dropped on us, an incredible unity especially among blacks and whites that seemed to flow over to people of all nations. We received a baptism of love for each other.

The special intensity of love for people of other races lingered in me for many months. Sometimes, naturally, we have to put extra effort into loving people who are different from us, who speak another language, or are from a different culture. This gift of love from the Lord was totally different—it was as though these differences only made the love stronger and better.

"Was I racist before?" I wondered.

That wasn't it—it was just that after this experience, my previous love looked weak and pathetic. The only reconciliation we will find together as individuals or as ethnic groups is found in Jesus Christ, who paid for our unity with His own blood.

"JESUS GETS WHAT HE PRAYS FOR"

While the planning team was not leading each evening of 10 Days (the host congregations were doing that), we did ask each host to give us five to seven minutes to share an update on what was happening throughout the city and share the vision for 10 Days.

I had been asking God for a way to communicate the essence of the promise of Jesus's prayer in John 17, "let them be one, just as we are one." I wanted to be able to tell people briefly, and in a way that was memorable, that Jesus's prayer was impossible, that it was completely scandalous for Him to pray this way about human beings, and yet the Father was going to answer His prayer.

And then, I hit on the essence of it:

"Jesus gets what He prays for."

That's it—Jesus is God's Son, and the Father is going to answer His prayer for us to be "one as He and the Father are one." It's going to happen—it just remains for us to get on board.

Over the years I've seen more faith released in the people of God for unity in the Body by this one phrase than by anything else. Let's live our lives in light of this truth—Jesus gets what He prays for.

10 DAYS AFTER SEVEN YEARS

The first 10 Days Boston was a resounding success both in terms of engagement and spiritual power. Thousands of believers in Boston had joined and participated and many lives were touched. A fresh sense of John 17 unity was released over the church in the city. As we concluded the final night with the "Boston Night of Worship," over 7,000 believers joined together singing songs to our great King. There was a fresh sense of hope and anticipation for what God would do in Boston.

Truly, God was beginning to fulfill His promises. A major city, thousands of people, and more than fifty local churches had just partnered in a ten day prayer event. And while I knew this was just the beginning of what God wanted to do, I rejoiced in this significant step forward.

For seven years I had been doing my best to follow Jesus and steward the vision. The road had been more difficult than I could possibly have imagined. And growth of the movement was slower than I foresaw. Still, after seven years, we had prototyped 10 Days in a number of different models, survived painful failures, and stumbled into extraordinary breakthroughs.

Personally, those seven years had been an intensive time of spiritual formation. I had barely made it through in one piece. However, in the process, I had learned so much about following Jesus—I barely recognized the idealistic young revivalist who had taken off in a car years earlier to spark a national revival. Emerging out of the wilderness, I was leaning on my beloved.

10 Days Boston was both the end of seven formative years and the beginning of a new era of growth and expansion. From that point on, we'd build based on lessons learned and models developed in those first seven years. It was time for 10 Days to spread around the globe.

PART TWO

A GLOBAL MOVEMENT

15

LEARNING HOW TO GROW (2012-2014)

STARTING in 2011, 10 Days grew from one location, to three, to twelve, to twenty locations by 2014. The vision was beginning to spread. This is the story of how God began to grow the movement.

The year 2012 was big for our family. Four years after sensing God calling us to Western Massachusetts, we finally moved from the greater Boston area into the land of Moody and Edwards. We had vision to start a house of prayer with local friends and within a few years, to see night-and-day prayer at the Northfield campus. That this vision seemed unlikely and impossible was no impediment. We were following Jesus. He seemed to only want to do impossible things.

In 2012 we saw small but important developments in 10 Days as a movement.

That fall, we had three city-wide 10 Day gatherings at the same time. The movement was beginning to grow. As I had discerned, the fall 10 Days was quickly outpacing 10 Days Pentecost as the major focal point for the year.

After leading another 10 Days in Boston, full of miracles, encouragement, and answered prayers, I reflected on the original vision, seeking the Lord for what was next. As I prayed, I remembered the vision of a map that kept getting bigger and bigger. I realized now was the time for the "map vision" to begin to be fulfilled. 10 Days was supposed to be happening simultaneously in cities across the United States and all around the globe. That was God's desire. But how would it happen?

BACK TO WHERE WE STARTED

In some ways, this was a return to where I began in 2005. However, this time I approached the prospect of expansion with more insight into God's ways. Proverbs 20:21 says, "An inheritance that is gained hurriedly at the beginning will not be blessed at the end." This would be a gradual process—we didn't have to win the whole nation in one year.

Also, there was another major difference from 2005. This time, we had actually done 10 Days. This was no longer theory—we had amazing stories to tell and years of experience and testimonies to draw on. The seed of the vision was ready to be sown far and wide.

BISHOPS AND UNITY CATALYSTS

While I firmly believed God was going to spark gatherings all over the world, I had no idea how to have multiple 10 Day prayer meetings at the same time. The three gatherings in 2012 had happened almost by accident.

I had personally organized 10 Day events in various ways. Now, I needed to step into a new role where I was primarily inspiring and teaching others to start their own 10 Days events.

As usual, I didn't know what to do and I was afraid. It was time to pray.

I asked the Lord to show me how to multiply a united prayer movement. The Lord spoke to me about two important types of people to look for as I shared the vision in fresh places.

"There are bishops, called to shepherd cities—these [bishops] are also [usually] pastors."

Here God highlighted the role of church leaders, most of them pastors of churches, who have a calling to a city, state, or region. Immediately upon hearing this from the Lord, I could think of many people who fit this category. Their business card might not say "bishop" on it, but God was using them to shepherd entire cities and unite the church in that region.

The Lord went on:

"There is also the new breed, those like [certain people you know well]. They have been called forth to establish John 17. They belong to the prayer movement. They belong to the whole church. Their love and faith that I will accomplish My prayer [in John 17] will cause them to endure to the end."

"As I call them, recognize and affirm them. You will hear the sound of your own calling in their voices. This isn't a movement of pastors, but of apostles of unity, sent to cities to establish My will and kingdom. They will be humble, be peacemakers, be joyful, be tenacious, and persevere in hope for every brother in Christ. They are not afraid, and not afraid to fail."

The Lord also told me that when I shared the 10 Days vision with this new breed of John 17 catalysts, it would be "received as an answer to their prayer" rather than perceived as a burden or as "one more thing." In other words, 10 Days was a strategy to help these people do what they were called to do—unite the Body of Christ.

Hearing this word stilled my fear and brought needed clarity. I now knew two types of leaders to look for in each new city. I knew the "Bishops" would usually not do the heavy lifting of organizing 10 Days; instead, their blessing would be important. The "unity catalysts," if I could find them, were the ones to run with it; they were the ones who had been asking God to show them how to unite their cities.

Building on my experiences on the North Shore and later in Boston, I saw how 10 Days could serve existing city-wide movements. Most cities have some type of pastors' network. The leader of this group is very often the "bishop," although that title is rarely used. I saw 10 Days as a type of "software" that could run on the "hardware" of existing unity networks in a city. 10 Days was intended to serve these networks and to advance their mission. I had seen that first-hand how effective that had been in just a few cities. Now it was time to release these gifts from God to more and more places.

REDEEMING THE TRAVELS OF 2005

As a new season of national vision casting began in the fall of 2012, God spoke about my first failed attempt in 2005.

He told me: "You thought you had failed in 2005, but I did not fail you."

The Lord told me that while nothing had happened right away, I had put "seeds" into the ground in 2005. These seeds were about to come up. In the Lord's eyes, even the worst season of failure in my life was not wasted.

"I am going to bring you back to specific places and even specific rooms where you experienced rejection and disappointment [in 2005]. This time you will experience favor with those same groups and in those same places—many of the same groups will now join in 10 Days."

God's re-framing of the failures of 2005 brought incredible hope. In December 2012, as I began traveling once again to cast vision for 10 Days, I found myself having meetings in many of the places I visited on the west coast in 2005, sometimes in exactly the room or coffee shop we had been in before. But this time, instead of rejection and indifference, people were open and wanted to do 10 Days. In some instances, ministries that had quickly brushed us off then now paid my travel expenses to come, share, and collaborate.

OUR PLAN TO GROW

In 2004, God showed me how spreading 10 Days would be as simple as getting in a car and talking to people. I still saw this simple strategy as what God wanted me to do. However, this time I tried to use more wisdom.

Multiple times a year, I would go out traveling, usually with a friend, sometimes with my kids, and share the 10 Days vision. I'd try to find the "bishops" or "unity catalysts" in a particular area.

As I traveled, I made friends with hundreds of amazing people. While this strategy wasn't producing massive growth, each year the number of cities involved in the movement steadily increased. 10 Days was growing at the pace of friendship.

NO MONEY, NO MARKETING, NO CELEBRITY

There are many ways that ideas, products, and movements grow. It was interesting to me that 10 Days was growing steadily and with almost no money, hardly any staff, very little marketing or social media presence, and no celebrity.

I'm not opposed to any of those things—in fact, I'd love to have them. However, that's not how the Lord led us.

We could have gone out, hosted a massive fundraiser based on some of our successes, and hired staff and an advertising agency to call the world to do 10 Days. However, every time I would ask the Lord about such things, He said no.

"Why don't you keep trusting Me?" I would hear Him say. "I like that."

I'm not prescribing it for everyone—I admire people who can get things done in a variety of ways—but this is how the Lord led us.

Often, we would have divine appointments with unexpected people as we traveled. Sometimes, new cities were added as God sovereignly called people to do 10 Days and then introduced us to one another. I liked to joke that our "marketing strategy" was simple: dreams, visions, and divine appointments.

Honestly, I was so accustomed to simply "following the Lord" on major decisions that doing it this way seemed completely natural and normal.

CONNECTICUT 2013

Late 2012, God specifically told me there would be an open door for 10 Days in Connecticut in 2013.

In early 2013, I was about to call Rick McKinniss, a friend and fellow collaborator for many years through the New England Alliance, to ask him about joining in 10 Days in 2013. Rick is a clear "bishop" type who has a special calling to unite leaders in Connecticut. However, as I prepared to call Rick, I felt the Lord say to call Gregg Healey instead. Gregg and I had met twice at that point, but we didn't know each other well.

When I called Gregg, it became clear why the Lord had redirected me. The Sandy Hook school shooting had just taken place in Connecticut, with many elementary children murdered in one of the nation's worst school shootings. God had impressed on Gregg's heart that repentance and prayer, a 2 Chronicles 7:14 response from the church, was needed in response to these kind of tragedies. He had been praying and asking God for a way to unite the church, focused on repentance and corporate prayer.

And then I called. Amazingly, it was just as the Lord had told me: "10 Days will be an answer to their prayers." As I got to know Gregg better, I realized he was one of the John 17 "unity catalysts" I was supposed to find and encourage. Right away, Gregg and I began a strong friendship that has continued to this day.

Gregg and Rick worked closely together as part of a movement called Impact Connecticut. A national prophetic voice had recently called Connecticut to do 40 Days of Worship throughout the entire state.

The invitation to 10 Days seemed to be further confirmation of this direction from the Lord to unite the state in worship. As the conversation progressed, it was decided that the 40 Days of Worship would start on the same day as 10 Days. 10 Days had been important in confirming the vision and there was a desire to partner together. However, there was confusion around messaging and branding—was this "40 Days" or "10 Days"? What was the right way to merge these visions?

A few months before the event began, Rick called me. He told me directly that the name "10 Days" would not appear in any of the materials for the 40 Days of Worship. While I was welcome to consider the 40 Days a "10 Days expression," this meant that people in CT would not really hear about 10 Days. Also, some of our major themes, including the call to mourning and the focus on the Lord's return, would not be part of the emphasis.

At first, this was hard for me to hear. At that point we had only seen three gatherings in 2012—this was our big success. I was trying to build on that and see a global movement emerge. The new effort in Connecticut was shaping up to be the largest expression to date, involving over 100 local congregations and thousands of people. I was trying to grow a global movement, and becoming a "silent partner" didn't seem helpful.

However, in a moment, those thoughts were totally overwhelmed by a powerful sense of God's anointing presence that landed on my head and extended to my toes. As the Lord touched me, I realized several things all at once.

First, it was right for me to submit to Rick and the leaders in Connecticut. They were the proper authority and were responsible to God for their decisions. I needed to agree with what they were sensing from the Lord. Not only that, but Rick and many of these leaders were my friends who loved me—they were for me.

Second, I saw how in the Kingdom it would be incredibly profitable to have the influence of 10 Days buried in this first year. It was the move of humility. While it seemed like it would slow our growth to not receive credit, I knew in the Kingdom, it would be an accelerant. As we often say, "in the Kingdom down is the way up." Helped by the Holy Spirit, this opportunity for humility filled me with incredible joy.

Finally, it clarified the branding issue for me in a fresh way and allowed me to live out a core value. We needed to have a name (10 Days) so that we could invite others to join and talk about what we were doing. However, our central focus was not promoting our name, but fostering unity among God's people and encouraging them to seek His face.

I whole-heartedly submitted to and agreed with Rick's decision. It was the right call. Since then, we've often had people copy, change, or modify 10 Days—or do something similar under a different name. It makes no difference what we call it; let's just seek the Lord.

STORIES FROM NEW PLACES

As 10 Days stretched to twelve locations in 2013 and then twenty in 2014, familiar stories of God moving emerged from new locations such as Manchester, New Hampshire; Hollywood, California; and Bellingham, Washington.

There were more than fifty churches working together in Boston, thirty in Manchester, one hundred in Connecticut, and thirty-five in Chico, California. Amazingly, the least Christian parts of the USA, the Northeast and West Coast, were leading the way.

TESTIMONIES

In Manchester, New Hampshire, a powerful new wave of unity impacted church leaders in the city. At the end of 10 Days, a layperson felt led to gather a few ministry leaders so they could discuss reaching their city together. He was expecting a handful of people might show up. Instead, more than fifty different ministry leaders came to the event, ready to work together to reach their city. What had been impossible before united prayer was now possible. The attendance and new openness to collaboration shocked everyone, and they attributed the unexpected result to answered prayer.

In Connecticut, the 40 Days of Worship initiative was a resounding success. I attended a pastors' meeting on the heels of the event. 150 pastors from around the state came out to spend the day in prayer and fellowship. I had been to similar pastors' gatherings in the past. Pastoral ministry is hard, and many times leaders come in empty, looking for a recharge. However, this event was the opposite. There was an incredible presence of God—recognizable as a spirit of revival. The atmosphere was electric, full of love, light, and power.

Yet there was something else present as well, something I had never felt before. There was a willingness to run together, similar to what I would expect from an army. These leaders were not only experiencing corporate revival, they were also in alignment and prepared to move forward as one. It was an amazing thing to behold—I felt as though I was finally seeing with my own eyes what I had been searching for over many, many years.

CRYING OUT FOR MORE

And yet, amid this incredible progress, a cry was welling up in my heart. Though we were seeing more and more locations, churches, and people participating in 10 Days, the incredible weight of God's power and glory that we saw at many of the Northfield retreats was not happening to the same degree.

Yes, we were seeing answers to prayer and unprecedented unity in many cities. The testimonies each year were incredible. And yet, I had seen much more powerful moves of God happen with smaller groups that had stopped everything to seek the Lord. We had seen stronger expressions of John 17 unity, outpourings of the Holy Spirit, and even transforming revival happen at these early 10 Day retreats.

I knew one of the major factors: almost no one was clearing their schedules and taking vacation time to seek the Lord. In the city-wide context, unlike a retreat, most participants were simply showing up for a prayer meeting or two in the evening. Most weren't joining all ten evenings, much less stopping everything to pray throughout each day.

I knew God wanted cities to stop everything to exalt His Son, Jesus. I knew that before cities would stop, individual believers and then entire city-wide church communities would have to stop. But clearly people were not grasping the message. It was so counter-cultural that people literally could not hear or understand what I was saying.

What God wanted seemed to be a combination of our Northfield Retreats and the city-wide 10 Days we had been doing recently. But getting more than a handful of people to stop everything for prayer was beyond my abilities. 10 Days was going wide and impacting cities, but the cry of my heart was that it would go deep. After almost ten years, I still had no solution for this problem. I was desperately crying out to God for an answer.

16

THE JESUS TENT (2015)

"I can't believe that I'm saying this because it's the busiest time of the entire year. But I'm going to say it anyway because I sense the Lord on it—I will spend five of the ten days with you in Wilmington, North Carolina."

It was early 2015, and my new friend from the south, Michael Thornton, was in the middle of a Holy Spirit swirl, one that was now sweeping me up as well.

He had just explained to me how God was miraculously making a way for them to put up a tent in Wilmington for 24/7 prayer and worship during the Ten Days of Awe. Somehow, I had just committed myself to be there for five days—something that made no sense to my natural mind since that was when I was most needed in New England.

Michael was a revival leader from North Carolina who was introduced to me as a "modern day George Whitefield."

I had cast vision for 10 Days that November in Wilmington. Michael explained what happened in the aftermath of my visit.

"I knew the Lord wanted us to merge the DNA of the 10 Days gatherings in New England with the 24/7 Ignite gatherings we have been doing in the Carolinas..."

The vision of 10 Days of 24/7 worship in an outdoor tent gripped Michael. After he prayed for the Lord to show him the exact location to set up the tent, the next day a young doctor he had never met contacted him through their website. The doctor shared how God had given him a vision of a massive worship event at Legion Stadium in Wilmington.

"[The doctor] saw worship team after worship team come and lift up Jesus. People with campers were pulling in and camping out and through explosive worship, miracles, salvations, and healings were breaking loose. Jesus so filled the atmosphere that people were getting touched everywhere."

Sensing this was God's chosen location, through a further series of miraculous events, Michael gained access to the grounds right outside Legion Stadium completely free.

Maybe you can see now why I was excited to go to Wilmington.

10 DAYS WILMINGTON: THE JESUS TENT

In 2015, 10 Days continued to grow steadily, to a total of twenty-five locations. While some places would join for a year or two and drop off, many were now in the habit of doing 10 Days annually. Of the twenty-five gatherings taking place, I didn't have to organize a single one.

This freed me up to travel to Wilmington for the first half of 10 Days. Even though I was the founder of the movement, I knew I was headed to Wilmington as a student. I was there to learn.

THE SCENE

When I arrived, I found a large, circus-type tent pitched in an open yard on one of the major streets in town, just in front of a medium-sized stadium. Campers and tents were pitched around the main location, just as the doctor saw prophetically, and dozens of people were milling around before the first night. Soon, a large, homemade barbeque pit was towed in and grilling commenced—over the course of 10 Days, the Jesus Tent would feed thousands of meals completely free.

While I was a little surprised by this—10 Days is a fast, after all—I had learned over the years to trust how individuals planning local gatherings are led by the Lord. If the Lord led them to eat hot-dogs instead of fasting, that was okay. It was also a tangible way of loving and serving the community that allowed thousands of people to experience the goodness of God.

As the 10 Days began, the tent quickly filled up. Hundreds of people from dozens of local churches came out for the evening sessions. The main session ran from seven to nine p.m., and sometimes featured a speaker, but always included a different local church leader from the city of Wilmington leading communion. The tent began filling up around five p.m. and then emptied out around eleven. During the peak times, from seven to nine, there were always hundreds of people present.

However, the evening sessions were only a small part of the Jesus Tent. Dozens of worship bands led worship 24/7 in two-hour shifts. Throughout the night there was low volume worship in compliance with city noise ordinances, all facilitated by a sound guy who seemed to never sleep. A core group of about sixty people had cleared their schedules and were totally consecrated to worship and prayer at the tent. Some of these people were camping in the parking lot, others were staying at local churches and ministries or hotels. Entire families had committed to this, and a pack of kids was running around and playing near the tent all day. Life was happening everywhere, but exalting Jesus 24/7 with worship and prayer was the central point, the "tent pole" around which everything else revolved.

THE POWER OF CONSECRATION

After a day or two, God's presence intensified. God was not only showing up from time-to-time; He was resting and remaining with us as we sought His face. The presence of God was thick.

I could see clearly how those of us who were set apart for the whole 10 Days, as opposed to just coming and going, were experiencing more of God together. While the evenings were amazing, some of the most powerful times with the Lord happened when fewer people were present, during the day and even in the dead of night.

One afternoon, an outside worship band led a set. As they stepped on stage, the tent had about twenty people present. All of us except the worship team had been living there, worshiping all day and night.

Often, worship leaders need to guide the people of God into worship. In this instance, worship was exploding from the people in the congregation who had been worshiping for days on end.

In fact, new songs of worship began emerging from the people on the floor, unamplified and unsolicited. I'll always remember the face of the worship leader, shaking his head, laughing, and wondering what was happening. The people were leading in worship because they had been with God.

Signs, wonders, and miracles—highly creative and unexpected—were breaking out all over the place. A spirit of Acts 2 generosity exploded, with people giving incredible gifts to each other left and right. At the end of John 20 and John 21, the gospel writer tells us that it would be impossible to record all the things that Jesus did because the earth could not contain the books. We started tapping into that reality in the Jesus Tent—too many amazing things were happening to keep track.

TESTIMONIES FROM THE TENT

I'll tell a few of the testimonies, but keep in mind this is only a small sample of what happened, and I'm sharing those that made a special impression on me.

A senior government official attended the first night and declared through tears, "I have never experienced love like what I just experienced here."

During a foot washing, as a woman had her feet washed, her broken foot was completely healed.

A man on his way to commit suicide in the middle of the night biked past the tent after finding the bridge where he was going to jump had been closed. Instead of killing himself, he met Jesus and was saved that very night.

A local man who was a contractor and ran a food pantry approached Mike Thornton. He was in tears recounting how God had touched him personally under the tent. This led him to ask Mike, "What do you need?" Mike mentioned they could always use water. Rather than delivering a few flats of water, the man said, "I'll deliver a pallet." Soon an entire pallet of bottled water was fueling nonstop prayer and worship, free of charge to all involved.

The city had been very concerned about homeless people breaking into and destroying the public bathrooms, so much so that they had almost not allowed their use. One night, someone forgot to lock the bathroom doors, and the homeless indeed broke in. However, rather than ransacking everything, they cleaned the bathrooms top to bottom.

Homeless people were being touched by the power of God—they were giving away their coats, their last food, all their money to other people even poorer than they were. The spirit of generosity was unbelievable!

A man who was saved asked to be baptized right away. The team had brought a baptismal, but it had not been filled yet. As the team explained to the man that the tank was completely empty, he continued to insist he be baptized right then and there. As he was still speaking, a firetruck arrived unsolicited and filled the baptismal font with hundreds of gallons of water. He was baptized on the spot.

God was pouring out John 17 unity and love on the Body of Christ in Wilmington just as we had experienced in our early 10 Days retreats.

THE POWER OF THE RETREATS TOUCHING A CITY

With all this happening, it slowly began to dawn on me that God was answering my prayer.

I had been longing to see the power, glory, and John 17 unity of the 10 Days retreats cross over and impact people at a city-wide level. What I was seeing in Wilmington was every bit as powerful as what we experienced in Northfield. With the help of Michael Thornton and the Jesus Tent, God was showing me a new model for 10 Days and for city transformation.

Also, I continued to bear witness to how powerful it was when people set themselves apart to seek the Lord for an extended season of time—the difference between those who just dipped a toe in and those who remained immersed in God's presence was startling. But even in this incredible atmosphere, most of the attendees were not quite there. It was still only a hungry few who could see the power of these extended, consecrated seasons of worship.

I also could tell certain elements of the vision were harder for people to understand. It was fairly simple for people to have a heart for revival. It was much harder for many to connect with the idea of "mourning for the return of Jesus." There was still more the Lord was looking for in terms of mourning.

This new level of fulfillment led me into praying for greater fullness:

"Thank You Lord; now give us entire cities stopped for 10 Days to seek your face like this. Give us entire cities stopped and mourning for your return just as you showed me."

While I could see that more needed to be done, my dominant emotion as I drove north to finish 10 Days in New England was wonder and gratitude. After eleven years of stewarding this vision, we were just starting to see how consecrated worship, prayer, and repentance could impact a city.

On my final night of 10 Days, back in New England, I found my mind wandering. I was getting distracted and was not very engaged as I prayed.

I began to apologize to the Lord: "I'm sorry for being distracted and not finishing well—this is your time." As I made my apology, I heard the Lord laughing at me. I saw in my mind's eye a grapefruit that had been totally squeezed of all its juice. He told me: "You've been poured out—there's nothing left to give." As He said this, I sensed His pleasure. And then, I saw a much larger, massive grapefruit, full and ripe. I knew this would be me in the future. The reward of giving our all to God and His people is that He expands our capacity to give, so we can give even more.

"Lord, pour me out for Your people." This was the deepest desire of my heart as 10 Days 2015 ended. It's also the type of prayer God is willing to answer.

17

RESTORE (2016)

AFRICAN PROLOGUE

IN March 2016, I traveled to Africa for the first time.

10 Days had continued growing steadily in the United States. We had twenty-five 10 Day gatherings in 2015. And we were now seeing the power of the Northfield retreats at a city-wide events. It seemed the vision was slowly unfolding.

I knew God wanted 10 Days to become a global movement. My hope was to share vision for 10 Days with believers in Africa. It made sense to me for Africa to be our first international location. I had always carried a special love for the people of that continent and had received so much personally from its godly men and women, people like John Mulinde of World Trumpet Ministries and Graham Power who started the Global Day of Prayer.

Instead of having an opportunity to share as I hoped, I found myself with seemingly endless opportunities to serve. Upon arriving, I discovered I was part of the prayer team for the large conference of about 700 delegates from every nation in Africa. We spent the days leading up to the conference in extended times of intercession. It turned out the worship group that had committed to lead during the main sessions canceled at the last minute. Suddenly, I was thrust into the worship band with my Nigerian roommate, who was the worship leader. Somewhat inappropriately, or so it seemed, I found myself playing hand drum with the band for a room full of Africans. Proof, if ever you need it, that God does not call the qualified but qualifies the called.

During the conference, a variety of things went wrong. Again and again, I found myself able to serve, whether fixing microphones, managing the sound system, running errands for the leaders, or serving delegates. However, contrary to my initial hope, I had almost no opportunities to share the vision of 10 Days.

In one of the last prayer sessions for the conference, off to the side in a small room, I sensed the Lord's pleasure in my willingness to serve. I knew it was the Kingdom way to wash the feet of the saints, and I sensed God's pleasure in taking the "low seat at the table." I heard Him say, "I am giving you Africa." That sounds like a big deal, but I knew what He meant. 10 Days had His permission to operate in Africa. He would give us growth there.

I flew home, happy with how the trip had gone, even though none of my hopes for sharing the 10 Days vision had been realized. All I had to show for my travels was a tiny whisper from the Lord in prayer. However, I knew the greatest in the Kingdom was the servant of all—God had opened doors for me to serve. If I kept my life on that trajectory, I could trust the Lord to call people into 10 Days at just the right time.

WHAT EVER HAPPENED TO NORTHFIELD?

In 2016, Northfield once again took a central place in the story. Here's what happened since we left Northfield in 2009.

At the early retreats from 2007-2009, God began speaking to many of the participants about His plan to restore the property back to its original intention. Many of us had the same vision for the campus to be a multi-organizational center of John 17 unity, 24/7 prayer, missions, farming, and even a place of refuge and divine protection during coming trials.

My entire family had stayed in New England and later relocated to western Massachusetts in pursuit of this dream. While it may seem strange to some, we were making costly decisions as a family because of a sense we would be part of reviving the property, and then establishing a house of prayer and multi-ministry center on the campus.

However, since the sale of the campus to the Green family for $100,000 in 2009, virtually nothing had gone according to plan.

The Greens planned to give the campus to a group called The C.S. Lewis College. However, after they failed to meet fundraising goals, the campus was taken back. In 2011, they were looking for a new group to receive the campus. *Christianity Today* published an article about Northfield entitled, "Who wants a free Christian Campus?" After all this effort, another deal for the property fell apart at the altar.

In 2013, Northfield was given to the National Christian Foundation by the Green Family. This was simply an intermediate move for tax purposes: NCF was tasked with giving the campus away to a qualified Christian organization. In 2013, I personally got in the mix with several partner organizations, drafting a collaborative proposal for a multi-ministry center. However, when one of our partners pulled out to make a run at the campus on their own, the collaborative proposal fell flat. None of the other proposals succeeded either.

By early 2016, the situation had not changed. The beautiful campus that Moody founded remained in limbo, as it had been since 2005, barely used and mostly empty. I suspected God's specific plan and calling on the property was behind the long delay and many false starts.

In late 2015 God began to speak to me: "Northfield is about to become very important again in this season."

One night, as I was falling asleep, I had a vision where the Lord told me, "I'm going to use you as a key to open this campus."

There were many other prophetic leadings and confirmations from our local team. And yet, I was more than a little hesitant. Northfield had been a major disappointment to me in the past. The pain of major disappointments, delays, and even betrayal by mentors and close friends while waiting for God's promises at Northfield was fresh on my mind.

ANOTHER DISAPPOINTMENT

At that time, we had a small but committed team of people who had moved to Western Massachusetts to start a house of prayer at Northfield. With all of us sensing God was shifting us there, we decided to take a step of obedience. Not having any other direction from the Lord, we decided to bring key leaders from around New England together to pray. That February, we hosted a small prayer gathering of about fifteen people on the campus.

I also reached out to the National Christian Foundation to check on the progress of their efforts to give the property away. I was thinking of submitting another proposal.

They made it clear to me that a deal for the campus was all but done.

"I can't tell you more about it until it's finalized, but don't bother worrying about it anymore."

The news filled me with deep discouragement.

At this point, I had been asking God to revitalize that property for eight long years. The journey had been incredibly perilous for me and my family. Constant financial pressure, painful conflicts, and previous failures loomed large in my mind. I had suffered and sacrificed so much in faith to see Northfield revived—could this be how it would all end?

Despair had latched on; I couldn't see a way forward.

Thankfully, God was faithful to bring encouragement from an unexpected source.

THE SOUND OF MUSIC DREAM

Gregg Healey and I had been friends for a while. However, we had never worked together on Northfield. As I was marinating in discouragement, wondering what in the world I was doing chasing this crazy dream for an old, abandoned campus, Gregg called me.

"I had a dream last night, and I think it was about Northfield."

This was unexpected.

In the dream, Gregg was in a Blockbuster video store. I called him while he was in the store and told him something on the phone. Immediately, he went up to the front register and rented a special edition of the movie *The Sound of Music.* It had five DVDs, with the middle disk of the five being larger and more prominent that the other four disks. As he received it from the clerk, he could tell that he had gotten there just in time.

He also learned that he could not buy the set, only rent it, and that the cost to rent it was $17.

As he rented and walked out of the store he could feel jealous stares from those who had wanted the disk, but it was too late. Gregg had received it.

"Does that seem like it has anything to do with Northfield to you?" Gregg asked.

I had no doubt the dream was about Northfield. Among other strange overlaps, the "five disk set" was a direct reference to part of our 2013 business proposal for the campus to be owned by four groups held together by a fifth "backbone organization." Gregg and I had not talked over this proposal at the time, so he was unfamiliar with it.

We went into dream interpretation mode, beginning to explore the other symbolism of the dream.

"Rent not buy. I think God is saying the solution this time is a rental, not owning the property." Gregg opined.

"Why seventeen dollars?" I asked.

"Sometimes the number seventeen symbolically means 'victory'." Gregg explained.

I had never heard that before. In fact, the number seemed completely arbitrary to me. After pondering it a bit more, I realized I referenced seventeen all the time when I spoke about "John 17 Unity."

"Could it be that John 17 unity is the currency that could allow us to rent the campus?" I wondered.

ROBERTO LEADS THE WAY

That March, Roberto Miranda, a long-time ministry partner and pastor of one of more influential churches in Boston, visited the Northfield property for the first time. As we walked and prayed outside in the cold with about fifteen other people, the Lord spoke to him about the property.

One of the central features of the campus is a large red-brick auditorium. Built in 1895, it seats over 2,000 people. It was built by Moody to accommodate the large crowds that would come for summer conferences. While the auditorium, along with the rest of the buildings, was closed, Roberto boldly walked right in through a door that was cracked open and gained entrance from a local maintenance person.

As Gregg and I followed, Gregg commented, "Roberto leads the way." As we stood on the same stage where Moody had preached many times, Roberto said what we were all thinking.

"We need to do a gathering here this fall."

JOHN 17 IS THE PRICE OF ADMISSION

Several months later, Roberto, Gregg, and I would gather in Boston with several other leaders of the Alliance. From what we could surmise, another deal for the campus had fallen through, the latest in a litany of near-misses.

Months later, we were still thinking about Roberto's utterance. We were convinced that God wanted us to host a New England-wide assembly there in the fall and that somehow this united gathering of the New England church was important if Northfield was to be reopened.

It was agreed that I would ask the owners to let us host 10 Days at Northfield and a regional assembly in the D.L. Moody Auditorium.

I knew from my earlier conversations that the owners did not want to host gatherings on the campus. Their mission was to give the campus away to a group that could steward it well, and hosting events did not fit within their assignment.

In short, I knew our proposal stood no chance. However, with the encouragement of Gregg's dream, the direction to "rent and not buy," and the understanding from the dream that "John 17 unity" was the price to rent, I was willing to make the call.

I decided to put the dream to the test—I would offer John 17 unity as the price of admission and see if they jumped at the offer.

My conversation with the owners went something like this:

"Our group, the New England Alliance, would like to host a gathering at Northfield this fall in the Auditorium, and do 10 Days of Prayer leading up to it," I offered.

"Lots of people would like to do that, but we're totally focused on the campus's future, not on hosting events there right now," came the expected reply.

"I understand that, and if possible we want to help toward that end. All of us want to see Northfield revived. Our group is a John 17 movement from all six New England states. Could it be that a united New England Church might be part of God's plan to open the campus back up again for ministry?" I put the dream to the test.

Silence.

"That's an interesting idea; send me a proposal in writing and let me get back to you in a few days."

After exchanging proposals and negotiating, they invited us to host five of the 10 Days of Prayer at Northfield, outdoors. We would also be permitted to host an event at the Northfield Auditorium on October 12, the last day of 10 Days. Gregg's dream had worked. We had an open door.

A CALL TO WILMINGTON

Now that the door was open, we had a new problem—how would we ever host half of 10 Days of Prayer outside? Who did we know who had a tent?

I called Michael Thornton in North Carolina and explained what was happening, before offering an outrageous proposal.

"Would you consider driving the tent up to Massachusetts and praying 24/7 for five days on the Northfield campus?" It was such a big ask, I couldn't believe the words were coming out of my mouth.

In 2015, Michael Thornton and the Jesus Tent crew had been blown away that so many people from Massachusetts had come down to worship and pray in North Carolina. Unbeknownst to me, they had committed themselves *in writing* to return the favor and come to Massachusetts to help us here. After Michael confirmed with his team, the Jesus Tent was headed north for Northfield.

It is incredible to have friends and partners in the Kingdom like that—people who will drop everything they're doing and travel long distances at their own expense to help others fulfill their God-given calling.

VACATION DAYS FOR PRAYER

Meanwhile, 10 Days was moving forward on other fronts as well.

That summer, I shared about 10 Days in Connecticut as I had done many times before. I cast vision for taking vacation days to seek God, stopping everything, and clearing our schedules for prayer with believers around the world. While I had shared this vision with thousands of people, it was simply too radical and countercultural for almost anyone to hear.

A young pastor named Luis Burgos was in the crowd that day and the message resonated with him. He was hungry to see a move of God and sensed the Lord stirring him to do 10 Days in Bridgeport, Connecticut. But would his people say yes to something as radical as taking their precious vacation time to pray? He was afraid to ask.

He returned to his church and shared the vision, leaving out what for him was the hardest part—taking 10 Days of vacation time to seek the Lord.

Immediately, after hearing this, his staff, who all had full-time work outside the church, said, "Pastor, if we are really going to do this, we need to start taking vacation days at our jobs." The stage was set and Luis, a bulldog of a leader, had the bone between his teeth.

That September, Luis gathered over seventy pastors from Bridgeport for dinner. They graciously allowed me to share the 10 Days vision for over an hour. To be honest, I was used to only having five to ten minutes—or at most thirty minutes—to share. With so much time, I was able to share many amazing stories about how God had moved in the past.

Two weeks later, he had me back with a new group of seventy pastors, and we did it all over again.

Our second gathering was only a week and a half before the start of 10 Days.

As we met that night, a new vision began to emerge prophetically right in the meeting. An enormous circus tent had been made available, and space had been granted by the city right next to the stadium in Bridgeport. 10 Days Bridgeport would follow the same pattern as 10 Days Wilmington—a massive tent next to a stadium, with 24/7 prayer and the partnership of well over fifty churches. The Jesus Tent was coming to Northfield, and what we witnessed happen in Wilmington was coming to Bridgeport.

RESTORE

By that August, the plan for Northfield was coming together.

We were calling the New England church to rally to Northfield, to be part of the "key" that would open the campus again, and release God's purposes in New England. It was going to be incredible. The "Sound of Music" was going to be heard once again on those rolling hills.

As this was happening, Cassi and I were completely out of money. A slow trickle kept coming in to provide for our daily needs, but we were behind on our rent and had received almost nothing for over three weeks. In addition to our own personal needs, the cost to rent the auditorium at Northfield was $7,000. We had nothing in the ministry account to put towards it.

After three weeks of having less than $100 in our bank account, Cassi let me know: "I've been patient, but you need to solve this now."

My wife is a very patient woman and full of faith, so I knew this was a sign I needed financial breakthrough...and soon.

Having walked with the Lord and seen many miracles of provision, I knew I needed to talk to Him.

I WILL PLEAD YOUR CAUSE

I told Him, "Lord, you know we have no money and are behind on our bills. I like working and I'd be happy to get an extra job to help pay the bills. I'm happy to move out of the area if you don't want to provide for me to live here—we are only here because of Your call. I'm also happy to start fundraising or asking for the resources we need for the Restore event, if that's what you want me to do."

The Lord spoke clearly and compassionately:

"Don't get a job...don't plead your cause. If you plead my cause I will plead your cause. You will not leave New England. You will not leave your present house."

He also spoke to me about how to move forward at Northfield.

He said this: "Northfield is a book. I want you to read this book page by page. Each page is a new surprise, a new revelation. You will know what to do on the present page. Some pages will delight, and some will bring fear and disappointment. Keep turning the pages. There is a happy ending. I am giving you that campus. Do not doubt and mark my words."

I knew God wanted me to "plead His cause," to publish what He was doing at Northfield that fall. And so, that afternoon I sent out a major email detailing the plans for 10 Days and Restore, making no mention of the financial needs. I had been planning to ask, but after God told me not to, I didn't mention money.

In response to that email, a Christian foundation responded back and let me know they were sending a check for $10,000 to cover expenses for Restore. Wow, that was fast! And yet, I still had so little money that just operating as a family was challenging.

"Lord, thank you—now what about our personal needs?"

The next day, a check arrived for $3,000 out of the blue. Shortly after, another $1,000 arrived. We were able to cover the back expenses we owed.

Once again, God had come through. As I declared what He was doing, He pleaded my cause and met our needs.

AFRICA JOINS IN 10 DAYS

I won't say I had given up on Africa; I just wasn't thinking about it. There was too much happening. Just weeks before 10 Days was to begin, I received a call from an American missionary named Carole Ward.

Her ministry was based in Gulu, Northern Uganda. Carole had seen incredible moves of God through prayer in one of the darkest parts of the continent. She had lived through a brutal war and seen God come through when her life was on the line.

Ironically, she had been looking to see that kind of prayer, unity, and repentance happen in America. I, on the other hand, was seeing it happen in America but was looking for an open door in Africa.

As Carole and I shared hearts, God used our conversation to spark the first African 10 Days in Gulu.

The Lord was giving me a down payment on what He had spoken that spring. Somehow, in His economy, obedience, serving others, and trusting the whispers of the Holy Spirit was the way to see a massive vision come to pass. His ways were so upside down from the world's ways, yet so much more beautiful.

AN AMAZING CITY-WIDE GATHERING

As 10 Days began in 2016, I was full of anticipation of what God was about to do. That year, thirty locations were participating; the movement continued to grow. Personally, I was helping pull off a 24/7 prayer meeting that would be half in Boston, half two-hours away in Northfield.

After years of 10 Days happening on the coasts, it was now taking root in the middle of the nation; places like San Antonio, Cleveland, and Denver. Several locations had established a rhythm of hosting annual 10 Days gatherings, with entire states like New Hampshire and Connecticut partnering in a state-wide strategy that included many different expressions.

A few days in, I began getting calls late at night from Luis Burgos who was leading 10 Days in Bridgeport. God was moving in unexpected ways, and he had questions. They had set up 24/7 prayer with over fifty churches buying in to the whole vision, and many people in the city taking vacation days off to seek the Lord together.

On the second night, they had about 150 people in their red and white, candy-cane circus tent. But by the third night, and every night after that, they had over 500 people in the evenings. The atmosphere was electric as Bridgeport experienced an unusual movement of united prayer.

I was able to attend one night in Bridgeport and was profoundly touched by what I saw.

In the pre-service prayer, about forty pastors and leaders from around the city prayed passionately together. The sense of unity was palpable. Luis and the team had thoroughly read our materials and were striving to make 10 Days a time of mourning and repentance, not just a moment of unity and exciting corporate worship. Spending time with the leaders, I felt they were honoring the vision of 10 Days better than any other city-wide gathering I had personally witnessed.

As the evening service began, there was a weighty sense of God's holiness and the fear of the Lord in the room. God was there and you did not want to mess around. I felt as though I wanted more than anything to repent and confess my sins to God, and yet I couldn't think of anything I hadn't already confessed. This profound weight of God's presence I knew was touching on the type of mourning and repentance that God was after from His people. That night, I felt I was seeing part of the vision of 10 Days come to pass for the first time.

LET THE CHILDREN COME TO ME

Meanwhile, on day five, our friends from North Carolina started to arrive. The Jesus Tent was pitched at Northfield, just a stone's throw from D.L. Moody's grave. There was a chill in the October air, so we borrowed a heating system to keep prayer and worship running 24/7 through the cold autumn nights.

Our friends from North Carolina were staying in dozens of locations, from host homes, to local churches, to hotels. More than sixteen people packed our home and even our yard. It was wild, with "all hands on deck" to honor Jesus and care for the needs of the saints who had come to minister to the Lord. The self-sacrificial, servant leadership of Michael and the entire team from North Carolina was incredible to behold, as they honored those of us in New England above themselves and served wholeheartedly in the place of prayer.

On the first night in the tent, I noticed my daughter Sabbath, who was just eight years old, leaping about at the front of the tent in an exuberant worship dance. She seemed totally transported—a shy little girl suddenly had no qualms about dancing in front of more than a hundred strangers.

Later that night as we were driving home, I asked her what had happened.

She told me her story,

"Well, I was dancing before the Lord and as I danced, I began feeling so much joy inside and it made me dance more and more and I felt like I was flying. And finally, the joy inside of me erupted and I started speaking in tongues."

"Wow. Show me," I asked her, and she obliged.

Seeing Sabbath encounter God powerfully that night was my personal highlight from that year. As a father, nothing was better than seeing my children walking with the Lord.

RESTORE

On October 12, we hosted the Restore gathering at Northfield. On a Wednesday afternoon, in the middle of the day, almost 1,000 people came to the Moody Campus, in the middle of nowhere. The gathering had multiple elements—worship and prayer continued outside in the autumn sun, filling the campus with a glorious sense of God's presence. Seminars and workshops were hosted in various buildings. As I walked around that day, I knew I was walking in the fulfillment of promises God had made me when I first came to New England.

The entire atmosphere was like a spiritual family reunion, with old friends who had not seen one another in years unexpectedly reunited. We concluded with the Restore Gathering in the historic auditorium with over fifty leaders participating from the stage and giving testimony to what God was doing in their cities and states.

As we entered the building, I knew we were walking in the fulfillment of Gregg's dream. There was a spirit of John 17 unity. The hills of Northfield were alive again with the sound of music. Moody's legacy was being honored and the campus was open at long last. Rarely in my life have I felt so proud and honored to be part of something.

In yet another remarkable confirmation of Gregg's dream, the total cost of our event at Northfield came to $17,000—almost to the dollar.

All of what was required had been freely given, without any offerings being taken or requests made. God had "pleaded our cause" just as He said He would.

Here, in a region of the United States known for being spiritually cold, an amazing movement of revival connected to our incredible history was beginning to flourish.

IT'S DONE

The next day, as we returned to clean-up, we ran into a group of leaders from the National Christian Foundation who were responsible for finding new owners for the campus. I shared our hope that the Restore event would be part of helping to reopen the property.

"It's done—we've finished the deal," they shared.

While the details of what happened would not be known for several months, there had finally been a breakthrough. After over ten years of being empty, the Northfield property would be used once again. In the mysterious ways of the Kingdom of God, our prayers had somehow been instrumental to opening the door. God had used us like a key to unlock the campus.

18

LIKE THOSE WHO DREAM (2017)

GO TO ZERO

THE 10 Days 2016 gathering was a significant step forward. With thirty locations participating, we were seeing steady growth year after year.

Even more important to me, we were starting to see dynamic, city-wide moves of God that had all the spiritual power of our early retreats. On a personal level, God's promises to me about Northfield as a place our family was called to serve—promises that had governed our family's direction for many years—seemed on the verge of coming to pass.

Despite these things, our local team in Western Massachusetts was disheartened. We all had moved to the region to see a house of prayer established at Northfield—a crazy dream, but a God dream.

Now, even after seeing the improbable Restore gathering in the Moody Auditorium, we still had no place for a house of prayer. After over eight years of carrying this vision and four years of working together, we were seemingly no closer than when we started. Financial challenges, delayed hope, health problems, and painful conflicts with brothers and sisters in Christ were wearing my team down. Key contributors moved out of the area and others pulled back from active involvement.

God had done great things in 2016, but our desired goal of establishing a house of prayer in Northfield had not come to pass.

As I wrestled with discouragement and loneliness, I received a word from the Lord:

"Go to zero," He told me.

Oddly, this encouraged me.

In the Kingdom, down is the way up. If we want to be exalted by God, we need to follow the way of Jesus who, as stated in Philippians 2, "became obedient unto death, even death on a cross." Jesus went to zero. The road to zero is the way to be exalted in the Kingdom. So, paradoxically, I was encouraged. God was sending me on the pathway to promotion.

In the moment, I interpreted this word to mean that all of our team would step back and Cassi and I would have no money. I would be alone and broke. That didn't sound so bad. This would, in fact, happen over the next months. However, I didn't fully understand what the Lord meant and what was about to take place.

THE NEW NORTHFIELD

In the winter of 2016-2017, the decision on Northfield had been announced. The campus would be split between St. Thomas Aquinas, a Roman Catholic "Great Books" college, and a new group called The Moody Center. I had mixed feelings about the decision.

"Lord, is this really what we have given so much of our lives for?" I wondered.

Some elements of the vision God had given us for Northfield were present in this new arrangement. For instance, it was a multi-ministry center. However, other important pieces were missing.

Previously, God told me the Northfield book had to be read page by page. I resolved to focus on what I could control and trust the Lord with the rest.

The upside of the new arrangement was that the Moody Center was open for business. And we were experiencing a lot of favor with them.

Now that Northfield was open again, we formed a plan for the fall with partners around the region—we would host an entire 10 Days at Northfield (inside this time) and conclude 10 Days with a four-day conference called "Restore and Revive" in the Moody Auditorium, featuring worship, workshops, and internationally known speakers.

THE PLOW OF SUFFERING

As I feared, in the spring of 2017, my local team went to zero. I felt more alone in Western Massachusetts than at any point in my journey. However, it comforted me, knowing this was God's plan, and it motivated me to pray for the Lord to assemble a new team.

In March 2017, I returned to Africa to visit the group in Northern Uganda that had hosted 10 Days in 2016. I knew God wanted to see 10 Days expand in Africa. I needed to meet people face to face and share the vision. The journey to Uganda was blessed, full of new friends and divine appointments with African leaders, many of whom continue to be friends and partners in ministry to this day.

While in Africa, I woke up early each morning long before the sun came up. Because we were right on the Equator, the hot days were only twelve hours long, so I would wait for hours on the porch of my hut, worshipping, praying, and drinking hot, instant coffee that surprisingly, was incredibly delicious.

One morning as I worshipped, I saw the Lord coming to me in a vision. He was pushing a plow that was clearly too big for Him and was struggling to move it on His own. This struck me as strange, since I usually envision plows being pulled, not pushed.

"This is the plow of suffering." He said to me. "There are not many willing to help Me with it. Would you help Me?"

As I heard these words from the Lord, a flash of panic and fear passed through my mind.

"The plow of suffering sounds horrible," I thought, recoiling in dread.

And then, following right behind the fear, an overwhelming sense of what Jesus had done for me filled my upper body with unspeakable joy.

"Lord, You gave Your all for me. How could I ever say 'no' to You?" I responded.

I gave Him my wholehearted "yes" in that moment, overwhelmed with gratitude and by the beauty of what He had done on my behalf. It seemed like the least I could do. For the rest of the morning, I wondered, "How could anyone say 'no' to this man?"

I wrote this in my prayer journal and didn't give it another thought for the rest of the trip.

HOLY WEEK

After I returned to the U.S., everything seemed normal. As usual, I didn't know what would come of my travels, but I was confident God had been with me. Seeds had been sown; now it was time to trust the Lord for a harvest.

After about two weeks, I began to have flu-like symptoms. Just when I thought I was recovering, they came again. My wife sent me to get some blood work at a local hospital. I barely made it home, having to pull over multiple times because of the severity of the illness. The next day, Wednesday, I was finally admitted to the hospital and diagnosed with malaria.

Throughout Thursday, my condition worsened. I don't remember much besides the constant pain. At one point, I opened my eyes and saw my mom in the room.

"What are you doing here, Mom?" I asked. She lived over 1,000 miles away.

I started to realize I was close to death. From what God had spoken to me, I felt I had much more work to do. It did not seem like my time to go. But my body was telling me I was dying. In that moment, I evaluated my life. I realized 10 Days would carry on if I passed away. I knew other elements of the ministry would also endure. I sensed my wife would make it and recover, even though it would be very hard on her. She was so strong. But when I thought about my six children, aged eleven to three, I realized they needed me. I couldn't leave yet—those kids needed a father.

It was Holy Week. I nearly died on Good Friday. The doctors later told me how close I came. On Easter Sunday, they cleared me to go home. Even though I was still very weak, I was alive. A Muslim doctor told me that of all the thousands of cases of malaria he had seen in Pakistan and India, mine had been the worst he had witnessed. He also told me that only God could have healed me—and that I had God to thank—not medicine, not him, not the other doctors.

As I left the hospital, I reflected on my experience in Africa with Jesus pushing the plow of suffering. I had walked the way of the cross and resurrection that Holy Week. Amid the pain, I felt honored to have been able to suffer with Jesus in that way. While incredibly difficult, I could see the hand of God all over it.

"Go to zero," God had told me.

"It's hard to go much lower than dead," I reasoned. I concluded at that point I had gone to zero, and it was time to look for God to do the impossible.

As it turns out, I was partially right. What would follow was an amazing season of God's promises being fulfilled. However, as I was soon to discover, there were even deeper depths than physical death on the horizon.

10 DAYS 2017: TRANSFORMATION IN THE USA

10 Days in 2017 would be the most powerful year to date. Thirty-five cities participated, including several new sites in Africa. It would be possible to write an entire book just about 2017, focusing on the testimonies of each location that participated. I'll focus on three threads of the story that I was able to witness personally.

BRIDGEPORT, CT

One word described Luis Burgos after his first 10 Days experience in 2016: hungry.

Bridgeport had experienced an incredible move of God, with many supernatural signs, salvations, and over 6,000 people attending their 10 Days event. However, Luis knew there was more. In particular, the lack of physical healings frustrated him. In 2017, he resolved it would be different.

Dozens of people were trained in healing prayer to prepare for 10 Days, and they began seeing regular miraculous healings at their church. In addition, he gathered worship leaders from churches around the city. He wanted to unite not only the pastors, but also the worship leaders of Bridgeport. As 10 Days approached, they were planning 24/7 worship, with over fifty churches and over sixty worship leaders partnering from around the city to exalt Jesus.

PROMISE FULFILLED AT NORTHFIELD

Somehow, I was back at Northfield leading 10 Days in the same room where we hosted our original 10 Day gatherings from 2007 to 2009. The joy of being back after so many years was like a liquid substance I could feel. Each step was a reminder I was living a miracle—a promise fulfilled by God, a promise that had taken ten years to come to pass. The journey had been incredibly difficult, but the pain only made the fulfillment sweeter.

As 10 Days began, it seemed each day the presence of God increased. On the fourth night, as we took communion, God's presence overwhelmed me. I got up and tried speak but found I couldn't use my tongue, so I just stammered a bit. While I knew I looked foolish, I was fine with it. The love and joy of God were all over me and it felt good. Aside from being tongue-tied (that was new), the experience was familiar to me.

The next evening, a few of us drove down and visited the 10 Days in Bridgeport. Entering the room, we saw about 400 people from many congregations around the city. The worship music was loud, so I sought out a seat on the side where the speakers weren't directly pointing at us.

REVELATION CHAPTER 4

Initially, I struggled to remain in the room. The music was so loud it was hard to think. But, as the time of extended worship continued, the presence of God grew heavy.

It was very similar to what happened the night before, but this was not joyful or playful. Instead, it was heavy, holy, and full of the fear of the Lord, the kind of presence of God Isaiah encountered when he said, "Woe is me, for I am undone." It was a Throne Room expression of God's presence, a Revelation 4 manifestation, the kind that causes the elders to fall on their faces and hurl their crowns to the ground.

In the initial 2004 vision, I had seen a city that stopped everything, a city where the heavenly Throne Room seemed to be present "on earth as it is in heaven." In the midst of this encounter, I realized I was seeing this happen for the very first time with my own eyes.

As the awe of God increased, I noticed I was filled with insight, revelation, words, and visions. The activity and gifts of the Holy Spirit were increasing dramatically beyond what was normal. I was supposed to speak, and I was receiving all these incredible insights and wonderful things to say.

But, there was a problem: the presence of God was so thick and strong I couldn't say any of what God was showing me. I was struck dumb, sitting in my chair, weeping.

A pastor got up on the stage to speak.

"How is he even standing up under the weight of glory?" I wondered as tears streamed down my face.

Immediately, he dropped to the floor and continued sharing face-down.

"That makes more sense," I said to myself through tears. The presence of God was so intense that standing on stage did not seem possible.

When it was my turn, I couldn't stand either, couldn't open my eyes, couldn't speak. My tongue was stuck just like the night before, but this time there was nothing funny about it; I sat on the stage, speechless and weeping. Eventually, I walked off the stage, sat back down, and cried the rest of the service.

This weight of His glory—it was almost painful, it was fearful, and yet the most beautiful, incredible thing in the world.

INCREASE

The next morning, back at Northfield, this powerful experience with God continued and increased for a third day. It started on the car ride with two of my daughters. I was totally exhausted, not thinking about anything when I found myself in God's presence, praying on the way independently of my conscious mind. As we entered our morning session and began to worship, the same, weighty glory fell in the room and increased.

As God's presence overwhelmed us, I had a vision that led me to repentance. In the vision, I saw that I had been living in a tiny shack, next to the ocean, yet an expansive mansion, and a continent's worth of territory was available to me.

I knew this shack represented the level of the knowledge and awareness of God I was living in versus what God had made available. I got up and repented publicly, with tears. "I don't want to live in a shack anymore," I sobbed.

My knowledge of God was miniscule. How could it be so small? I sat and wept, overwhelmed by the majestic holiness of God. Our morning prayer time was three hours long, but it felt as though a week was crammed into those three hours. Afterwards, many on our team were totally exhausted, undone by the power of God that overwhelmed our bodies.

I was reminded of the experience of Thomas Aquinas shortly before his death where he received a revelation that so completely overwhelmed him, he never wrote again or spoke of it. He only said, "All I have written seems like so much straw after the things that have been revealed to me." That's how I felt by noon on Monday. I was undone.

"Have I even known the Lord up to this point in my life?" I wondered to myself as I collapsed and fell asleep.

FIJIAN TRANSFORMATION IN THE USA

Meanwhile, the weighty presence of God kept increasing in Bridgeport as well. Each day, it grew thicker and heavier. At the conclusion of seven days, the packed worship space in Bridgeport was at a tipping point.

That night, Luis Burgos had a strange vision. At first he passed it off as the product of an overactive imagination. He saw a massive demonic principality, much larger than the building they were meeting in, made up of soil from the Bridgeport region, with a large hammer walking into the parking lot where the meeting was being held.

He thought to himself, "Luis, this a bad time to be imagining comic book stuff."

As he closed his eyes and tried to pray, he again saw this giant demon made of dirt with a hammer preparing to strike the building. As this was happening, He saw a little angel with a tiny sword block the blow as it was about to fall. The tiny angel was struggling to hold the hammer back from hitting the roof.

As he saw this, he heard the Holy Spirit say, "Send reinforcements to the roof."

Luis thought to himself, "This is probably just my imagination—but if it is God, I want to be obedient."

He went to one of his associate pastors and didn't tell him anything about the vision. He simply said, "There's some spiritual warfare and I need you to take three others and go pray on the roof."

The four men didn't flinch at this odd request and went right up to pray.

After sending them up, he promptly forgot about the four men on the roof.

Shortly after, he heard this from the Lord:

"What I break tonight breaks forever."

At this point, the weighty presence of God shifted and the oil of joy broke forth in the room. From 9:30 p.m. until midnight, more than

400 people danced continuously in the joy of the Lord, shouting and celebrating as a city-wide church.

"WHAT I BREAK TONIGHT BREAKS FOREVER"

The next day, the four men found Luis.

"Pastor, we have to tell you what happened."

Luis suddenly remembered that he had sent them to pray on the roof. Breathlessly, they shared a remarkable story.

Once the men got to the roof, they decided to pray in tongues from the four corners. As they did so, one of them had an open-eyed vision. In the experience, the Spirit of God descended on the roof and the man saw an open portal in heaven, like a fiery tornado touching down to the earth. Through this tornado of fire, enormous angels began descending from heaven, angels who "looked like they had been working out for all eternity for this very moment." As they descended, they struck the earth with their hands and each one overturned the earth for a mile around where they struck the ground.

"What is does this mean?" the men asked.

The Holy Spirit answered, "What I break tonight, breaks forever."

As the four men regrouped in the middle of the roof, they heard the Lord say, "Because you've honored My word, you can ask whatever you want from Me and I'll do it for you." Then all four were knocked out by the power of God for over an hour.

Two of the men were brothers.

While they were flat on their backs, one of them silently asked the Lord, "I want my father to see me serving in ministry." Their father had died several years earlier and hadn't lived long enough to see him step into his calling. This young man had a vision while he was on his back.

He saw his earthly father among the saints in Heaven. The Lord Jesus took him to a window in Heaven and opened it for him. As his father looked down, he saw his two sons lying on the roof and began to rejoice over them in Spanish, saying, "My sons, my beloved sons are doing the work of the Kingdom."

Once the four men revived, the brother who had the vision said to his brother, "I need to tell you what God showed me while we were out." The other brother replied, "No, I need to tell you what I saw."

Both brothers independently had visions from the Lord about their father that were identical in every detail.

A TRANSFORMATION STORY

What happened in Bridgeport that year followed the pattern of transforming revival seen in the Fijian Islands and 10 Days Northfield 2008. After seven days of God's presence increasing, there was an outpouring on the eighth night, where multiple people independently heard from the Lord, "What I break tonight breaks forever."

Also, multiple people saw prophetically that what God was breaking had to do with the physical land around Bridgeport. Luis Burgos saw a demonic entity made of dirt, and the roof team saw the angels striking the dirt. God was speaking through these experiences that He was "healing the land" in that area. The eighth night was the evening that "God came to town," manifesting His presence with incredible supernatural signs and a Holy Ghost dance party that could not be suppressed or contained.

AND AT NORTHFIELD...

While God was moving in unusual ways at Bridgeport, something similar was happening at Northfield. Hundreds and then over a thousand people gathered at the D.L. Moody Auditorium for the Restore and Revive Conference.

With keynote speakers like R.T. Kendall, Chuck Pierce, and Heidi Baker, and a powerful sense that God was doing something special, followers of Jesus flocked to Northfield just as they had in D.L. Moody's time. The Moody Auditorium was filled once again with passionate worshippers of Jesus.

As I witnessed everyone flocking into the Auditorium, I couldn't help but think of Psalm 126:

"When the Lord brought back the captive ones of Zion; we were like those who dream."

It had been a ten-year road to get here, but this journey of faith had finally resulted in seeing an ancient well of revival come back to life. It was electrifying to watch people encounter the Lord in that space.

The glory of God increased and overflowed in a dynamic revival atmosphere. On the eleventh night in Northfield, the presence of God was unbelievably strong. Chuck Pierce began to prophecy that we were experiencing a first-fruits of the revival God was preparing to pour out on America. It was truly a taste of Heaven on earth. I remembered how in Moody's time, people referred to the summer conferences as "Heaven on earth." The past was becoming present before our eyes.

On the final night, Heidi Baker, the blond, Pentecostal Mother Theresa of Mozambique, shared powerfully how God was knitting us together as a quilt in John 17 unity. The room was experiencing a corporate encounter with the Lord, but I couldn't fully engage. At that point, I was physically, spiritually, and emotionally spent. I needed to rest. Despite this, I couldn't have been happier with how I had spent my life. It was an honor to serve the people of God.

FROM DEATH TO DREAM FULFILLED

Several weeks after 10 Days ended, it happened. The Moody Center, the new group that now owned a third of the Northfield Campus, was opening a space for us to host a house of prayer at Northfield. And because God had assembled a new local team, we were ready to start immediately. Just months after "going to zero," our local team had re-assembled with many new people and was stronger than ever.

I was taken back to the formative outpouring of the Holy Spirit in 2008, those early days when God began speaking to us about how Cassi and I would be involved in what He was doing at Northfield. I remembered how He showed me that Northfield would have multiple ministries with distinct functions, that it would be a place where the "tribes come together," where missionaries would again be sent to the ends of the earth, and of course, that there would be 24/7 worship and prayer at the center of it all.

Somehow, through many trials, we were at the beginning of the fulfillment of this vision to revive the Northfield campus.

Everything we had been through was worth it to get to this point. Truly, we were "like those who dream." The Lord had done great things.

19

"I COULD HAVE SUFFERED MORE" (2018)

REVELING IN GOD'S FAITHFULNESS

THE autumn of 2017 was one of the greatest triumphs of my life. 10 Days had been instrumental in releasing a corporate taste of revival for New England. Finally, after years of work, we had seen a "Fijian style" transformation story in a western city, Bridgeport, Connecticut. Most important to me, the ten-year journey of faith to see the Moody Campus revived was paying off.

After years of radical faith, overcoming obstacles of every kind, our house of prayer was hosting prayer meetings at Northfield twelve hours a week.

While we didn't own anything at Northfield, we were experiencing incredible favor with the Moody Center. Clearly, God had set us up to partner with them. They blessed us by allowing us to use the space for prayer and we were blessing them by drawing all kinds of groups to Northfield.

And, we had plans to expand. 2018 would be bigger and better, with more events at Northfield including a student conference in the spirit of the Student Volunteers and an even larger Restore and Revive event. I saw nothing but blue sky on the horizon.

Amid all the growth, we had one significant problem. There was a conflict with some of our ministry partners in Restore and Revive. After trying everything possible to work things out, we had to part ways with them, a breach that was painful.

Notwithstanding this situation, things were looking up. Never before had I experienced a season of so much favor and growth.

"I COULD HAVE SUFFERED MORE"

As I reflected on my life to that point, it seemed like an endless series of crises and trials since I said "yes" to giving everything to Jesus.. I had no inkling when I started how hard it would be to follow Him. I wanted to live a life like the people I read about in the Bible—somehow I hadn't fully considered how hard their lives were. And yet, it had been worth it. I had arrived at the point of seeing God's promises to me at Northfield fulfilled. It appeared the good times had no end in sight.

As I meditated on this, I had a strange realization.

"I could have suffered more," I thought.

No matter how difficult the journey had been, I knew in my heart that I could have endured more, I could have given more, I could have waited longer for God to fulfill His promises. When we stand before the Lord on judgment day, no one will say "I wish I had given less for you." All of us will realize that what we've sacrificed for His sake was pitiably small in comparison to what He's done for us.

Although what I had endured had stretched me to the breaking point, part of me knew I still had more to give and that I would regret it if I didn't give the Lord my all. After all, He had given His all for me.

As I said this to the Lord, another part of me was thinking, "You are completely crazy to say that."

I was not in the market for more difficulty or suffering; this was not a "martyr complex." But I knew it was true—I could have suffered more. As I had this realization and prayed this prayer, I had no idea what was ahead.

"NOTHING YOU DO WILL WORK"

That May, we hosted a 10 Days Summit at Northfield. Participants from around the nation and the world poured in for four days of worship, prayer, and powerful teaching. We rejoiced in the now familiar sense of John 17 unity that saturated our time together in the very room where I had first tasted this supernatural oneness. God was moving, growing the 10 Days movement in amazing ways, just as He said He would. I was so thankful.

The level of favor we experienced with the Moody Center kept increasing. It was clear they wanted to partner more closely with us, and they appreciated how we were bringing so many people to Northfield. Opportunities for our future together seemed endless. The door was open and opening wider.

During the Summit, Brian Alarid, founder of *America Prays*, shared a word from the Lord that greatly impacted me. Years before, the Lord had spoken to him:

"Brian, when I want to show favor to you and exalt you, it doesn't matter what strategy or plan you use, everything you do will work."

That was exactly what I was experiencing. Everything I touched seemed to prosper. But it didn't end there.

"Brian, when I want to humble you, it doesn't matter what strategy or plan you use, nothing you do will work."

It was hard to remember what that felt like—I had to think back to 2005 and how our first attempt to do 10 Days had completely flopped.

Brian shared the Lord's heart on how the operation of grace works. It's not about our methods. It's about God's grace working in us. The word made a strong impact on me. However, little did I know how significant the second half of the word was about to become in my life.

A HOUSE OF PRAYER IN MOODY'S HOUSE

At the end of the Summit, we officially moved the House of Prayer into the D.L. Moody homestead. This was where Moody had lived from 1879 until his death. Somehow, I now had Moody's study to use as my personal office space. I pinched myself. How could this be? The goodness and favor of God was overwhelming.

In just over a year, I had gone from zero and almost dead to promises fulfilled and daily prayer in Moody's living room.

As May concluded, I had a time of listening to the Lord that would prove significant.

"You've become dull in certain areas through constant use," He said as I saw a dull, circular saw blade in my mind's eye. "I want you to step back for a season of sharpening and preparation for more."

This seemed impossible. "How can I step back during this season filled with significant work?" I asked.

He responded, "Your situation will be fundamentally transformed within four months."

I could only imagine at the time this meant something wonderful was about to happen. However, the word would prove to be both accurate and unexpected.

A HARD SUMMER

As we ramped up ministry preparations that summer, the wear and tear began to show. My health was poor and I was in chronic pain. At the same time, I was under pressure from almost every direction.

Our young adult conference did not go as well as expected—there was limited interest and unexpected conflict with several key leaders. Preparation for Restore and Revive was not going as well as in the previous year. We assumed that we'd see more interest in 2018,but as the event approached we had less than half the number of participants registered as the year before. And yet, our costs were twice as much. Our financial situation was a major point of stress as we approached the conference—we were approximately $40,000 from breaking even.

For reasons I could not understand, the favor we were experiencing with the Moody Center seemed to evaporate before my eyes. Had I done something wrong? At the same time, our local team of volunteers began to split into factions. In a ministry built on unity, conflict, gossip, and back-biting were now a major problem. The ongoing conflict with our previous partners continued to fester. As 10 Days neared, I struggled to sleep through the night as these cares and concerns weighed heavily on my mind.

A week or so before 10 Days, I opened the mail and read a letter from the IRS asking for thousands of dollars in back taxes. I couldn't help it—I laughed out loud. Everything that could go wrong was going wrong.

And that's when it hit me. I was doing all the same things I had done before that worked. Except this time nothing was working. It had nothing to do with my strategies or methods. God was humbling me.

As 10 Days began, it was clear I was living out Brian's word in a very real way—God had decided to humble me.

LEANING INTO HUMILITY

I resolved to do my best to lean into what God was doing instead of resisting it. If nothing was going to go as planned, I might as well submit to God's plan as best I could, recognizing this discipline was His goodness to me.

That year we had forty cities doing 10 Days. God moved in significant ways. However, for me it was the hardest 10 Days since 2005.

There were great moments of prayer, worship, and fellowship, but personally, everything was overshadowed by the painful humbling I was experiencing. I did my best to lean in and humble myself. In prayer, I spent most of my time lying on my face. That's where God's presence was.

As I continued to seek out ways to humble myself, the lingering conflict with our previous partners over Restore and Revive continued to trouble me. In prayer, I determined since in their view we had wrongly taken ownership of the event from them, the best thing to do was to simply give it to them. I didn't know if we had done something wrong. We tried to act with integrity every step of the way. However, it seemed that was the best thing to do. It was certainly a way to lean into humility. I talked to my ministry partner, Roberto Miranda, and we agreed. On Yom Kippur, 2018, we gave up our claim on the gathering that had borne such amazing fruit.

KEEPING THE SHIP AFLOAT

The next four days of Restore and Revive were very challenging. While many wonderful things were happening, including an anointed emphasis on racial healing and reconciliation, I couldn't enjoy it. Hanging over my head were all the debts that needed to be paid. Meanwhile, the divisions that had crept into our team had reached a breaking point. We were attempting to administrate a large conference with a team that had completely fractured.

I didn't know how it had happened, what I could have done differently, or how to get out of the situation. Our ship was taking on water and listing to one side. I was just trying to keep it afloat until the end.

In my heart, I felt the death sentence. I could clearly see that our previous favor with the Moody Center was entirely gone. I didn't know the cause. Had I done something wrong, or was it just business? Although nothing had been said, I knew the House of Prayer and everything we had been working on was about to end.

I had known God was humbling me, but the loss of what He promised me at Northfield, a promise I had pursued faithfully for over ten years, was more than I could bear. I could not emotionally or intellectually understand what was happening. The pain was too great. It seemed I was losing everything I had given my life to obtain—and I only cared about it because God had told me to do it.

How could He lead me to pursue an impossible dream, give me a taste of fulfillment after ten years, and then allow it to be ripped away? How could He allow this to happen?

20

AN EXTREME PRUNING (2018-2019)

THE AFTERMATH

I WAS destroyed.

For years, I had been zealous to see Jesus's incredible prayer in John 17—"let them be one as we are one"—answered. I had been pushing the limits of what was possible in God, traveling as a pioneer in undiscovered regions and calling others deeper.

Now, as I looked inward, I found no such ambitions. In fact, as I attempted to talk to God amid this devastation, my prayer was simple:

"God, save me from going to hell."

On the inside, I could see I was going to hell. Take the soul of the worst criminal you could imagine—I knew I was no different. I had been stripped bare.

Far from dreaming big dreams, I was simply crying out to God to save me from the person I had become and the punishment I deserved.

I was wracked by bitterness and resentment at those who had hurt me, stabbed me in the back, and hated me for no reason.

But the most painful loss of all was this: the story of my life no longer made sense. I had been walking, in extreme faith for ten years to see Northfield revived. Finally, it had happened—the vision had started to come to pass. We had a house of prayer in D.L. Moody's living room.

And now, just as suddenly, it was all over. How could it have happened? How could God have given me a taste of promises fulfilled after ten long years, only to strip it away. It was worse than if it had never happened. It was a much worse death than almost dying. Apparently, there are lower places than zero.

October was a time of deep despair. In addition to the loss of a prophetic vision that had motivated more than half my adult life, I had financial debts both at Northfield and to the IRS. Shame was layered on top of pain. Our small organization might have to file for bankruptcy.

Meanwhile, my problems were "holistic." When I visited the doctor, tests showed I had Lyme disease. The doctor looked at my bloodwork—some of my levels were those of a seventy-five-year-old man, not a young man in his mid-thirties. After malaria, I had never fully recovered. I was overweight and chronically ill.

By the first week in November, I had been in a downward spiral for six weeks. Each day was a bit worse than the previous day. I sat down with David Sparkowich, one of the pioneers of the Northfield house of prayer. We had partnered together for five years. I explained where I was at—I was in a bad place. I wanted to be faithful but wasn't sure how much I had to give. It was good to have a friend in that moment.

For reasons I don't fully understand, that moment was the bottom. From then on, things began to be a little better every day. But I had gone down a long way—it would take more than a year to fully recover.

LOSING MY PLACE IN THE STORY

I had no frame of reference to understand what had just happened. I had pursued a vision I believed was from God for ten years. He had showed His faithfulness time and again and done many miracles. The vision started to come to pass. How could He now allow it to be taken away? My story with the Lord no longer made any sense to me.

It was too painful for me to think about or try to figure out. Sometimes I was angry at God or other people about it. However, mostly I wasn't blaming God as I had in the past—I knew that was a dead-end—I was just in pain.

I decided to put the entire Northfield experience into an "I don't know" box in my mind. I didn't have the ability to understand what had happened or the inner resources to even think about it directly, but I needed to recover and work on strengthening what remained.

ECCLESIASTES

At that time, my friend Roberto Miranda was in a similar place. Both of us had held strong hopes for Northfield that were disappointed. We were both working through multiple conflicts and even betrayal from different people we loved deeply.

We had lunch together, and as we licked our wounds, Roberto mentioned how God was speaking to him through the book of Ecclesiastes. Immediately, I knew the Lord was speaking to me through Roberto. Before this time, I hadn't seen much value in Ecclesiastes, aside from highlighting what life is like without Christ. However, God began speaking to my heart through that book in new ways.

Having lost so much, the Lord began re-orienting me toward the good things that remained. Ecclesiastes states there's nothing better in life than to enjoy your wife, your children, and your work. I still had so much to be thankful for, including the best things in life. Losing so much I had worked for made what remained seem that much more precious.

Ecclesiastes says, "Do not be excessively righteous or overly wise. Why should you ruin yourself? Do not be excessively wicked…why should you die before your time? It is good to grasp one thing and not let go of the other." This type of thinking had never made sense to me before, but now I was beginning to understand it.

I was concerned I was being "excessively righteous" in my financial affairs. Following in the footsteps of one of my heroes, George Mueller, we had lived for years with radical financial faith, and seen more miracles of provision than I could remember. And yet, I had few earthly possessions of my own, no savings, and no inheritance to pass on to my children. Since I moved to New England, I had never had a savings account. I began crying out to God to remedy our lack even if it meant handling our finances differently in the years to come. I had no idea what that would look like, but new prayers were forming in my heart.

I also realized that in pursuing the spiritual depths and God's promises at Northfield, I had somehow lost sight of the basics.

I wasn't in love with the Scriptures anymore. My health was poor. I had entered into unwise agreements, often declaring "God is in this," and pushing forward relentlessly instead of resting in the Lord and allowing Him to do things.

I resolved to do whatever was needed to get my health back. I also rededicated myself to personal prayer and Bible study and took steps to strengthen my marriage. It seemed that if I could just get a few of these simple things right, everything else would work out fine. In my work relationships, I made a new commitment to act with pure motives and exercise greater care in close partnership. Our ministry developed new standards of accountability to limit exposure to debt in the future.

I had also learned an important lesson about myself. Management was not my forte. I asked God to give me a team of pioneers, entrepreneurs, and self-starters.

LOSING NORTHFIELD

Just before Thanksgiving, we received news that the House of Prayer at Northfield, our last remaining partnership on campus, needed to vacate the premises. I had been expecting this and had already mourned. By this point, I had bottomed out and was doing better each day. And this was the mercy of God, because as I was healing, my partner David went into the same depths of mourning and questioning. We were soul-sick in the extreme, but we took turns. Praise God for fellowship in suffering.

GOD'S MERCY IN THE DEPTHS

While I didn't understand what had happened, and the pain was strong, time and again God's mercy would break in.

During this season, I would receive calls almost weekly from friends and acquaintances I had not heard from in a long time.

"How are you doing?" I would ask.

"Actually, not great," they would respond.

"Well, I don't want to sound cruel, but that's actually kind of encouraging."

Calls kept coming in from people in almost identical situations. They too had been leading significant ministries, pursuing prophetic vision over many years, and seeing the beginnings of promises fulfilled. Then, like me, what had been thriving inexplicably collapsed and they were left holding the bags and scratching their heads. I wasn't the only one whose life with God no longer made sense. The fellowship in suffering with people I admired somehow made everything a little better. While I still didn't understand, I could see I was in good company.

On one particularly difficult night, I cried out to God with a lamentation from Psalm 88:

"For my soul is full of troubles...I am counted with those who go down to the pit; I am like a man who has no strength, adrift among the dead, like the slain who lie in the grave....who are cut off from Your hand. You have laid me in the lowest pit...Your wrath lies heavy upon me and you have afflicted me with all Your waves. You have taken away my friends, you have made me an abomination to them..."

The next day, I gave a revival history tour to a group that was passing through. As they prayed over me to thank me for the tour, they began praying Psalm 88—just what I had lifted up to the Lord all night.

Tears streamed down my face. God saw me. He heard me. His mercy kept meeting me in the depths.

CAN WE LEAVE?

In this time of loss, for the first time since we had moved to New England, I was ready to leave. I asked the Lord if we could leave the area now that the Northfield dream was dead.

Although I was in a lot of pain, and I wanted to run from God, I knew running was worthless. I might disobey out of spite for a moment. But later I'd just come back to following Him—why add to my pain by being disobedient?

Cassi and I told our children we were considering moving to another part of the country. The entire family joined together in prayer.

"Lord, do you want us to relocate? Can we leave Western Massachusetts? New England? Can we relocate somewhere closer to family, or just closer to more believers?"

My heart thrilled at the thought of moving back west, of being closer to vibrant Christian communities, or being closer to family in the middle of the country.

And yet, to my disappointment, God wanted us to stay put. Same house, same church. Everything was staying the same.

"Okay, if the Lord wants us here, we will stay." I wasn't even upset about it. After so many years, how could we stop following His voice? Where else could we go?

FORGIVENESS OF DEBT

In February 2019, my friend Milan Homola invited me to Minnesota for a personal prayer retreat. Milan is one of those people who I never want to say "no" to, even when it involves going somewhere colder than Massachusetts in February.

Our retreat was a precious time together as friends, and a great time with the Lord. While I had done my best to forgive at each step, I could tell there was still work to do. I wrote down a long list of people who had harmed me, some quite deeply, and forgave them, releasing all offense and holding nothing against them. God and I did business; it was an incredible reset.

Jesus teaches that if we forgive others the debts they owe us, our many debts will be forgiven. Just a few days after this intentional act of forgiveness, our significant debt to the IRS was canceled and our remaining debt for the Northfield events was paid. I had forgiven others, and now God had literally forgiven my debts. It was an incredible enactment of the Lord's words, "If you forgive others, your own debts will be forgiven."

In the early part of 2019, my soul, my body, my emotions, my close relationships, and my spiritual life were all starting to flourish again. The Lord spoke to me about what had happened—He called it "an extreme pruning."

AN UNEXPECTED ENCOUNTER ABOUT ABORTION

As my recovery continued in earnest, our family had a two-week vacation in Florida.

On our first night, after getting the kids to bed, I was eager to dig into my vacation reading. I was going to re-read *Crime and Punishment* by Dostoyevsky. Nothing like a heavy Russian novel to help put your own sorrows in perspective.

Sitting outside on the porch of our hotel, I couldn't believe how warm the air was. I was ready to relax and enjoy myself.

And yet, unexpectedly, Holy Spirit began to speak to me about something completely unexpected: abortion in America. Nothing was further from my mind.

As the Lord shared His heart with me, I began to be very afraid. His anger regarding the killing of innocent children was burning.

He showed me that night how He judges nations just as He judges people, based on their own words.

Because the Declaration of Independence declared, "We hold these truths to be self-evident, that all men are created equal that they are endowed by their Creator with certain, unalienable rights, that among these are Life, Liberty, and the pursuit of Happiness," our nation had suffered a horrific Civil War because we permitted slavery, a clear violation of the right to liberty and the equality of all men.

Abortion was similarly serious to God because it violated the equality of all people and their unalienable right to life. This was our founding declaration before God, and He was holding us to our own words.

"What the pro-life movement has done until now is not sufficient for what's next," I heard Him say. It was clear to me that a more forceful and costly stand for life was needed. Also, I knew this response needed to be more unified and have a greater spiritual depth. It would take a miracle to overturn Roe v. Wade, the court decision that made abortion a legal right in all fifty states. As this encounter went on, I was increasingly gripped by the fear of the Lord. I have rarely been more terrified of God's righteous wrath.

After about an hour, the experience lifted, leaving me shaken.

The rest of the vacation was more what I expected—rest and fun with the family. But I continued to ponder the experience in my heart. "What could this mean?" I wondered.

A NETWORK LEARNS TO BE AN ORGANIZATION

As 2019 wore on, I found myself investing more in 10 Days than ever before. I had virtually no remaining local responsibilities and I found I had a lot more time and mental energy to spend investing in key relationships and strategic thinking.

For the first time, I invited a group of nine to be elders in the movement. To be honest, I had been so focused on mobilizing city leaders that I had not thought about this basic step. It was now clear that expanding the leadership base was an important step as we prepared for greater growth and fruitfulness.

10 Days has always functioned as a network. It became clear that to grow we needed to become a better organization.

Networks are flat, voluntary structures with multiple connections. Organizations are hierarchical and structured toward completing certain tasks. While 10 Days was a beautiful network, we needed to grow as an organization, to establish a new website, better resources, clearer vision, and a team to serve all the locations currently involved.

Most individuals in churches are used to functioning in organizations. They have to learn to do the network thing; for instance, it's hard for organizations to understand how giving things away outside the organization is useful. As a John 17 catalyst, I was a natural network thinker. Learning how to build organization was like learning a foreign language.

In 2019, heeding the counsel of friends like Luis Burgos, Corey Unger, Pia Jo Reynolds, and others—people who think very differently from me—we started growing our organizational structures without losing the core values that had caused the network to thrive.

After years of growing by five locations a year, 10 Days grew from forty to seventy cities in 2019—the largest percentage of growth we had seen since the earliest days.

As 2020 approached, I was seeing the wisdom of the extreme pruning God had brought me through.

Rather than mourning the loss of Northfield, I was experiencing relief at having less burdensome responsibilities, and the joy of living without the relational conflict that had marred those amazing years. I still didn't understand what had happened, but I remembered what He said to me years earlier—the Northfield book had to be read one page at a time.

Just as He told me, God had changed my world in September 2018. Although at first it devastated me, I was beginning to see good fruit produced from this extreme pruning.

21

A NEW AZUSA? (2019-2020)

IT was a lazy summer Saturday in August 2019.

We spent the day celebrating the birthday of my youngest son and riding horses at our friend's farm. My thoughts were far from anything work related—it was a day to rest and enjoy.

That afternoon, a friend sent me what seemed to be a random text.

The message contained a first-hand account of a prophecy of William Seymour, the founder of the Azusa Street revival that started the modern Pentecostal movement.

> "Sometime in 1910, Seymour just stood up on the stage, took the box off his head and started prophesying. He said in about a hundred years there would be another revival like Azusa Street. Only this time it would not be in one place it would be all over the world. There would be a return of the Shekinah Glory and the miracles. This revival would not be with just one person or just pastors. It would be with everybody in the Body. This time the revival will not end until the Lord returns." (*True Stories of the Miracles of Azusa Street*, by Welchel and Griffith)

I was familiar with this word, sometimes called the "hundred year prophecy" of William Seymour. I did not know why my friend had sent it to me right then. We hadn't talked in several months. I glanced at the message but didn't think much about it.

THE AZUSA STREET REVIVAL

As the afternoon wore on, I found myself inexplicably drawn back to the quote.

As I knew from history, the Azusa Street revival started during a ten day prayer meeting.

After just a few days of prayer together at a home on Bonnie Brae street in Los Angeles, the Holy Spirit was poured out on this small group and many of them began speaking in other languages, including Hebrew. A woman who didn't know how to play the piano sat down and began composing spontaneous songs to the Lord, singing in many languages and, just as incredibly, playing the piano skillfully. A day after this outpouring on the group, William Seymour himself received "the baptism" and started speaking in other languages.

Over the next several years, the Azusa Street revival would serve as a catalyst for the modern day charismatic and Pentecostal movements. Thousands poured into a stable on Azusa Street to encounter God in a new way as miraculous signs, remarkable healings, and an all-pervading sense of the love of God were overwhelmingly evident for three-and-a-half years.

Keep in mind, the gift of tongues at that time was very rare among believers. Perhaps only a few dozen people world-wide were using this gift in 1906. Contrast that with today, where there are hundreds of millions of Christ-followers who use the gift of tongues in prayer, not to mention the other gifts of the Spirit. All those hundreds of millions trace their spiritual ancestry back to a little ten day prayer meeting at the Bonnie Brae House in Los Angeles.

These reflections on Azusa Street sparked a question.

"Do you like William Seymour more than me?" I asked the Lord.

I asked the question tongue in cheek. I had done dozens of 10 Day prayer meetings at that point. While we had seen many remarkable things, we had not yet seen an outpouring of the Spirit on the level of Azusa Street. Seymour did one 10 Days of Prayer and didn't even make it halfway through before revival broke out. Why was the Lord making me work so hard?

He answered my joking question with a serious reply:

"I'm putting more pieces in place this time."

120 IN 2020

This answer resonated with William Seymour's word about a greater outpouring like Azusa Street taking place all over the world, in many places at the same time.

And then it occurred to me—what if 10 Days was part of the fulfillment Seymour's prophecy? Could it be that God wanted people around the world to do exactly what Seymour was doing when revival broke out at the Bonnie Brae House in Los Angeles?

Seymour's prophecy continued to grow in me. What if we could see Azusa-type, 10 Day gatherings of fasting and prayer not just in one place, but all over the globe?

The number 120 from the upper room account in Acts 1 gripped my thoughts. What if instead of 120 believers in the upper room as in Acts 1, we could see 120 upper rooms around the globe, filled with believers seeking God's face "continually" and "in one accord"?

As this idea occurred to me, I found myself drawn to the number 120,000. What if 120,000 people would give themselves to praying in this global upper room, consecrating themselves for fasting and prayer like the Azusa pioneers?

Immediately, my inner critic rose up.

"120, 120,000, why are you obsessing over these numbers?"

In my spirit I heard the Lord say, "Read the last chapter of Jonah again."

I grabbed my Bible and opened it to the book of Jonah.

As a biblical precedent for 10 Days, I often reference both the "upper room" 10 Day prayer meeting in Acts chapter 1, and the story of Ninevah found in the book of Jonah. Ninevah is the clearest biblical example of a city that stops everything to repent and pray. In sharing about 10 Days, I would often say that 10 Days is "the upper room meets Ninevah."

Somehow, I had never noticed the parallelism built in the passages themselves. There were 120 people in the upper room. There were 120,000 in Ninevah.

A vision was building in me for 2020—could we see 120 cities host an upper room meeting, with 120,000 stopping everything to pray and seek the Lord?

Throughout August and leading up to 10 Days in 2019, this vision kept growing in me. For the first time, I just wanted to finish 10 Days 2019 so I could focus on the next year. I knew 2020 was going to be transformative.

A NEW PATTERN THIS YEAR

On the first day of January, 2020, I woke up with an incredible feeling of joy and anticipation:

"I was born for this year!"

There was a sense of divine calling and destiny as the year began—somehow everything I had gone through until now had prepared me for 2020. God's extreme pruning had left me feeling strong and ready to run.

I usually take time at the beginning of the year to listen to the Lord. This time of listening often provides direction for the entire year.

For instance, in 2017, the Lord told me to do everything we had done in 2016, but to grow and expand it. I did exactly that, basing my work on the previous year, but expanding and developing it more.

In January 2020, the Lord told me the opposite:

"Don't do anything you did last year again just because you did it before. You need to hear from me specifically before you do anything. There is going to be a new pattern this year."

For four years, we had hosted a 10 Days Summit each spring. The Summit was our best tool to share the DNA of the movement with new leaders and keep us relationally connected. It shocked me when the Lord said, "It is okay not to do a Summit this year."

As I looked at our 2020 calendar, I saw we were already planning to do 10 Days of 24/7 prayer online via Zoom leading up to Pentecost as a way of engaging our international partners.

"Well, I guess the 10 Days Pentecost on Zoom could take the place of our Summit?" I thought, even though it seemed strange to consider sacrificing an in-person event for a virtual one.

MOBILIZATION

Growing from 70 cities to 120 cities in one year was a massive leap. As I shared the vision with our team, it was clear to us that it would be impossible apart from His grace.

While I was counting on God to come through, I wanted to do my part in obedient faith. I was on fire to share this new vision.

My plan for 2020 was to travel half of each month and visit every state in the U.S., mobilizing 120 cities into a global upper room. In January and February, I did just that, traveling throughout the southern U.S. and West Coast.

GOD CONTINUES TO PROVIDE

I landed in San Diego in February 2020 exhausted and hungry from a long day of travel coast to coast. As I paid for a rental car, reality crashed in: Once again, I was beginning a trip with no idea how I would pay for everything I needed to do.

There was a significant gap between what little I had and the large sum of money I would need. Since I was hungry and tired, I knew I was more prone to discouragement.

"I wonder what the cheapest place to eat in San Diego is?" I thought. "I've been in this situation so many times over many years. How long do I have to live like this?" I was getting ready to throw a real pity party.

The presence and voice of God broke in. "I want you to go someplace nice to eat. I am providing for everything on this trip; I am covering everything."

In a moment, all my unbelieving reasoning was turned on its head. I felt courage rise in my heart. God had brought me this far. I am a man of faith. He will provide once again. I will see and bear witness to His goodness.

I found a delightful spot near my host home and had a delicious meal. It was definitely not the cheapest food in San Diego. Nothing had changed outwardly, but inwardly I had assurance—all would be well.

Sure enough, after several days of reminding Him of His promise, everything that was needed for my travels came through. I was able to give generously to others along the way thanks to God's generosity to me.

HONORING THE FATHERS

While in Los Angeles, I knew I needed to visit an important place—the Bonnie Brae House and the grave of William Seymour. It was in this obscure little house that the 1906 Pentecostal outpouring began. After trying in vain to arrange a visit, I decided to just show up. Providentially, the caretaker was present and let me in to pray. I lay on those wooden floors that had held the 1906 ten-day prayer meeting and asked the Lord to let me play a part in fulfilling what Seymour had prophesied. I sensed it was time to go, and as I rose to my feet, my host appeared to usher me out.

I traveled from there to the site of the Azusa Street building. Unfortunately, the barn where the outpouring was hosted had long-since been torn down. A simple plaque marked the physical place where an outpouring of the Spirit began that has affected almost every Christ-follower since; even those who have rejected it.

From there, I traveled to a large cemetery. After wandering lost for some time, I finally found where William Seymour was buried.

William Seymour, the one-eyed black man who "died of a broken heart" because of the divisions in the budding Pentecostal movement.

William Seymour, the man who endured rejection from his spiritual mentor because of his race with a forgiving and excellent heart.

William Seymour, a man of sorrows and acquainted with grief, just like His Master.

William Seymour—God remembers what you prophesied, and so do I.

As I drove away, a thought occurred to me:

"Wouldn't it be amazing to have 10 Days at the Bonnie Brae House in September?"

CITIES STOP

As I traveled up the west coast, rumors of a strange new virus from China were impossible to ignore. As I landed in Portland, Oregon, news came that authorities had identified the first confirmed cases of the novel coronavirus in the Pacific Northwest. My wife joked that I had given it to them.

The joke hit a little too close to home. I had been sick on the trip with a strange cold that caused me to completely lose my sense of smell. I had never experienced anything like it. Like many others, I may have experienced Covid-19 before there were any confirmed cases in the U.S.

Personally, I wasn't afraid of the virus. It was just a distraction. I had no intention of slowing down my travel plans—I had 120 cities to mobilize.

In March 2020, I drove to New York City to begin a week-long series of meetings on the East Coast. My plan to visit the forty-eight contiguous states was intact. After my March road-trip, I would have visited twenty states.

As I entered New York City with my son Melchizedek, the roads were empty. Normally, the city was a traffic nightmare, but today we were practically the only car on the road. Something unprecedented was happening.

While having lunch with a friend, the few people who were out seemed to speak in whispers. As we were about to leave, the radio informed us that starting the next day, all restaurants and public accommodations would be closed. We could hardly believe our ears. New York City, the global hub of finance and culture, was shutting down.

That afternoon, I returned to my host home with dear friends Grant and Hallie Berry. I was still planning to continue my trip south, but then, one after another, everyone began canceling. Everything was truly shutting down. I was suddenly aware how far I was from home at what felt like the end of the world. I needed to be with my family.

As cities shut down, the questions started pouring in.

"Jonathan, this is what you've been talking about for years. Is this what you saw?"

It was clear to me this was not exactly what the Lord had shown me. I had seen cities shutting down to turn from sin and worship Jesus. However, I felt this was a foreshadowing, a natural fulfillment of a greater spiritual reality that was yet to come. While I didn't clearly understand what it meant, one thing was plain: our world would never be the same. I also wondered—what if more people had responded to God's invitation to stop cities and repent? Would a Nineveh-like response have averted this disaster? Questions like that were above my pay grade. My job was to keep inviting people to do it and keep loving people. I only knew that after sixteen years of talking about it, cities were finally stopping.

DISRUPTION

As the days went on and normal life was turned upside down for weeks and then months, like all of us, we experienced fear. What was coming next? The early emergence of masks was shocking—what were our fellow citizens thinking, feeling, or saying behind the masks? One of the biggest disruptions was having to cancel my travel plans. How would I ever mobilize 120 cities without meeting people face-to-face?

However, despite these challenges, we felt incredibly blessed. As believing Christians, we had been expecting trouble in the world, and trusted God, not the world systems, to bring us through. God had led us to live in a rural area on a small farm. We could grow much of our own food and had plenty of space for the kids to run and play outside. He was shielding us in the day of trouble.

So what if I couldn't travel? I would work more on the farm, grow food, slow down, take long walks with my wife, read and study, and enjoy the unexpected respite.

GOOD IDEA LORD

As interactions with others moved online, I marveled at what the Lord had told me at the beginning of the year. Normally in March, I would have been deep in planning two in person events for April and May. Because of the word of the Lord, I wasn't even thinking about it. Instead, we had 10 Days of 24/7 prayer on Zoom already scheduled for the end of May leading up to Pentecost Sunday.

While some of my plans had been upended (like everyone else's), God had also strategically positioned us to thrive amid the pandemic.

PANDEMIC'S BENEFITS

Within the global prayer movement, the pandemic had an immediate, unifying effect. Suddenly, incredibly busy leaders were free and could connect from around the globe instantly. I was meeting respected leaders and heroes of prayer on Zoom; people like Graham Power from South Africa, who founded the Global Day of Prayer, and Mike Bickle, founder of the International House of Prayer.

With the crisis, our corporate availability, humility, and desire to work together were higher than I had ever seen. As someone who had contended for the answer to Jesus's John 17 prayer for years, I felt I was seeing global prayer networks align in a way that would make that possible for the first time in my life. Not only that, but as work stopped and fear ramped up, people were interested in prayer as never before.

During this season, Cassi and I also experienced a sea-change in our finances. For the first time in the fourteen years since we had moved to New England, we opened a savings account. Even in a global trial, God was pouring out benefits.

PANDEMIC STRUGGLES

While I was seeing greater encouragement among the prayer movement during the pandemic, this was not the case in every part of the church. On a call with pastors from around the Northeast, I heard an endless parade of discouragement as they wrestled with how to serve their people during the pandemic. Many were so discouraged they were contemplating quitting. Also, many well-known prophetic voices in the church were coming out with blatantly false predictions. Unfortunately, these public pronouncements were a source of dishonor for the church, especially since people were seeking prophetic encouragement as never before.

Many parts of the church were hurting even as other parts were thriving. As Jesus taught us in the parable of the house built upon the rock and the sand, times of testing reveal if we have built upon His words or on another foundation. The pandemic was shaking us all, causing some things to fall apart, others to be shored up, and revealing stability in unexpected places.

10 DAYS PENTECOST

God had interrupted my plans to travel the nation in 2020, but I soon found that using Zoom to meet people around the world was a far easier way to mobilize prayer. The biggest problem for 10 Days had always been that it was too hard to shut down everything to pray for ten entire days. Now, everything was shut down, so the idea didn't seem so strange. The pandemic had shaken everyone out of their previous mindsets and they were open to the Lord in new ways.

In April and May 2020, we pulled together a 24/7, 10 Days expression leading up to Pentecost on Zoom. With believers around the world leading prayer in many different languages, and with almost forty different teachers sharing, we saw a massive surge of new people connecting to the movement.

The palpable sense of God's presence in the Zoom prayer room was incredible.

While praying online had its challenges, the biggest advantage was that we could easily join hearts with brothers and sisters on the other side of the globe. One of my great joys was serving the Francophone West African group each night as a tech facilitator. I listened in the background, sitting on my couch until I was called upon to help in English, enjoying prayer in a language where I could only make out a word or two. During the turmoil of a global pandemic, God was causing His church to truly become "a house of prayer for all nations."

As 10 Days Pentecost ended, I heard familiar testimonies: The presence of God during 10 Days resulted in new breakthroughs of love for one another. Miracles, salvations, and answered prayers were common. John 17 unity was poured out with many tasting it for the first time. But now, the nations were experiencing it together in one place. As person after person testified to receiving an outpouring of love, one for another, my heart overflowed with joy.

Shortly afterwards, as I caught up on the news, I learned protests and even violent riots were taking place in the U.S. and around the world in response to the police killing of George Floyd. Suddenly, racial tensions in the U.S. were at an all-time high.

The juxtaposition was striking.

We had just spent 10 Days experiencing the nations, languages, and races of the world being united by the Holy Spirit at a level many of the participants had never experienced before. We had seen people from dozens of nations fall in love with one another. While tens of thousands hit the streets because of racial injustice, in the hiddenness of the upper room, we experienced the solution to the world's pain. Not rage and resentment, but worship and washing each other's feet. The solution to racial division wasn't protests in the streets—but rather a protest to heaven, calling out to the only man who will ever unite the nations in peace, Jesus Christ; asking Him to send His Spirit in our midst, and to come quickly Himself.

22

THE GLOBAL UPPER ROOM (2020)

As June 2020 began, the challenge of mobilizing 120 gatherings in the middle of a pandemic was starting to set in.

I was meeting more people over Zoom than I could have ever met in person. While people were happy to talk, everyone was afraid to plan anything, especially for in-person gatherings. Many churches still were not meeting at that point, and pastors were asking, "How can we go from not meeting all summer to hosting a 10 Day Prayer meeting?"

However, some leaders were sensing an opportunity for bold action. My friend Rick McKinnis in Connecticut heard the Lord saying, "Go big or go home." This was not a time for half-measures. One solution that fit the pandemic guidelines was a familiar one for 10 Days: meet ing outside in tents. Slowly but surely, commitments for new gatherings began trickling in.

THE RETURN

Prior to the pandemic, Kevin Jessip and Jonathan Cahn felt led by the Lord to host "The Return." Capitalizing on the meaning of the Hebrew word "Teshuvah," which can be translated "repent" or "return," The Return was a national solemn assembly scheduled during the Ten Days of Awe on the National Mall in Washington, D.C.

Kevin and I had known each other for several years. We had connected over our shared calling to the Days of Awe and our shared sense that America desperately needed repentance and revival. Historically, 10 Days had often partnered with a large, culminating event. As we moved from spring to summer, it seemed as though these two movements needed to come together. But how did they fit?

It's important in leadership to surround yourself with people who are both compatible and different. I found such a person in Grant Berry, a former businessman, entrepreneur, and Messianic Rabbi. He's an Englishman who lives in New Jersey. To say we have different backgrounds is an understatement, but what we have in common is a calling to John 17 unity.

Grant and Kevin had become close friends and the planning process for The Return was experiencing all kinds of challenges. They needed prayer support. Kevin asked Grant if 10 Days would be willing to serve as the intercessory prayer team for The Return.

When Grant shared this idea with me, I was not initially excited about it. It did not seem to be a good fit. When you have a prayer ministry, often people will ask you, "Could you mobilize a bunch of people to pray for what we're doing?" I knew our primary role was not to be an intercessory support team for different ministries.

"Grant, that's the wrong fit for us. Besides, we should be partnering with The Return to mobilize cities to pray during the Ten Days of Awe," I told him.

He was not deterred.

"Jonathan, pray about it. And trust me—this is the Lord."

Even as he said those words, I could sense I was wrong and he was right. God was calling us as a network to serve The Return in prayer. When we partner in the Kingdom, it's always important to come as a servant. Serving one another is the pathway to greatness; as it turned out, this was a perfect way for us to help. Thankfully, Grant recognized what the Holy Spirit was doing even when I couldn't see it.

Being part of The Return team was a joy for Grant and me. The entire group was motivated and professional, advancing a very complex project on schedule in the middle of a global pandemic. It was really an honor to be part of the team.

The Return faced incredible obstacles that summer. In a year where most large public gatherings were canceled, The Return somehow avoided that fate after numerous close calls. Most seriously, just weeks before the event, Kevin nearly died of Covid-19 before miraculously pulling through. I'm glad we were there to serve in prayer and play a small part in this significant national Solemn Assembly.

YOU NEED TO MAKE IT HAPPEN

In late August, less than a month before the start of 10 Days, I had hit a wall.

For the entire year, I had done everything in my power to mobilize people for 10 Days. After almost a year of work, we were stuck at seventy confirmed locations, the same as 2019.

I knew God had sparked this vision to call 120 locations. I knew God wanted a Global Upper Room, but I also knew that there was nothing else I could do to make it happen. On Monday night, August 17, I was deeply discouraged. I had given my all, but it was not enough. In desperation, I cried out to God:

"Father, I've done everything I know how to do. If you want 120 cities this year, You need to make it happen." I was done.

The next morning, I checked my email.

Much to my surprise, city-coordinator applications were flooding my inbox. By the end of the day, our number of city-coordinator applications had doubled. Over the next week, hundreds of applications continued to flood in.

I had no idea what changed—I had come to the end of my ability, and then God came through. As we later found out, several large Christian organizations had gotten our information from The Return and sent it out in their email blasts, leading to a flood of new contacts wanting to host 10 Days of Prayer events.

Within a few weeks, we had over 300 applications to host events. God had made it happen, but now we had a new problem—we were drowning in new contacts but didn't have the people available to follow up with them.

My suspicion was that many people applying to lead a 10 Days event didn't have any idea what they had signed up to do. So, we needed to contact each person, find out who they were and if they were genuinely interested, and then provide relevant connections and resources to help make their 10 Days event a success.

It was a funny situation, much like the disciples who fished all night, caught nothing, and then when Jesus showed up, found their boats sinking because of the catch.

I had been in despair because of too few people engaging—and now I was in trouble because there were too many. Thankfully, a friend from New England, Joellen Putnam, reached out.

"Jonathan, I know you're probably good and have a great team working with you but is there anything you need help on?" she asked.

I laughed out loud, and quickly caught her up on our predicament.

Joellen stepped in, took charge, and soon had us back on track. Her competence, courtesy, and organizational skills saved the day and were a striking example of God's provision in that season.

120 CITIES: FROM VISION TO REALITY

By September 7, almost two weeks before the start of 10 Days, we confirmed 120 cities would be joining. It was an incredible feeling. God had said it and now a year later, it was a reality.

I remembered back to 2007, when God told me to "call 120 [people]." His faithfulness over the years in that moment was overwhelming.

All in all, we confirmed over 155 locations in 2020, including 122 in the United States and 33 around the world. The Global Upper Room had become a reality in the middle of a global pandemic.

God also heard our prayers regarding several significant locations. At the beginning of the year, I had asked the Lord for 10 Days gatherings at the Bonnie Brae House where the Azusa Street revival started, and Herrnhut, Germany, where the Moravians hosted their 100-year 24/7 prayer meeting. I even asked for 10 Days to take place in the White House.

Two of those prayers were answered directly, as 10 Day events were scheduled at Bonnie Brae and in Herrnhut. I was a little frustrated that we hadn't confirmed a 10 Days at the White House. I guess I felt pretty sure God had heard that prayer. As it turned out, maybe I was right. The White House was about to play a central role in the story.

10 DAYS 2020

As the first night of 10 Days began, I was with my children at a 24/7 prayer tent near Hartford, CT. I was excited to launch 10 Days with two of my dear friends, Rick McKinniss and Matthew Rudolph.

As we were about to start, I received a text from Luis Burgos in Bridgeport.

"You won't believe what just happened."

"What's going on?" I asked.

I was expecting him to say there was a significant manifestation of revival, healings, or miracles. 10 Days was beginning, and I was expecting God to move.

"Ruth Bader Ginsberg just passed away," came the unexpected reply.

The shocking news of the passing of a Supreme Court justice just months before a presidential election caught me by surprise. I knew she was Jewish. Somehow, it seemed appropriate for her to have passed on the Day of Trumpets, the first of the Ten Days of Awe. I also knew that as one of the liberal justices on the Supreme Court, she was one of the votes keeping Roe v. Wade from being overturned. What could this mean?

We had not prayed for her death or wished her ill in any way. In my prayers for her, I had asked that she would do justice and be convicted regarding righteousness. However, like many millions of believers, I had prayed regularly for God to overturn the Roe v. Wade court decision. For each of us, our days are in God's hands. Clearly, God decided it was time to take her on the first day of the Ten Days of Awe. The door was now open for a new a new Supreme Court Justice—Lord willing, one who would reverse our national agreement with death.

INTERCEDING IN THE CRISIS

The fast that year was intense for both Cassi and me. We were in the middle of a global pandemic, living in a sinful nation coming apart at the seams, and crying out to God for relief from a plague. Our need for God's intervention was desperate and undeniable. We stood together, as husband and wife, and led our family in humbling ourselves before the Lord.

The solution as we saw it was a global, end-of-the-age revival that would never end until the Lord returned, just as William Seymour prophesied. We were pleading with God for mercy in the midst of judgment.

Halfway through the fast, I felt very weak. As I looked at the days ahead, I saw a demanding travel circuit, from Connecticut, to Boston, to Washington, D.C., and back to my home in western Massachusetts, all in just two days. I was worried I wouldn't be strong enough to finish the course.

As I arrived on the Boston Commons to pray, a friend put a hand on my back and said, "I feel strength in you." Instantly, I felt God's strength begin to fill me. Yes, there was strength in me for this. I remembered January 1. God had been preparing me my whole life for this year.

THE RETURN

I arrived in Washington, D.C. very early on Saturday, September 26, 2020. After months of online interactions, it was surreal to be part of a massive crowd of hundreds of thousands on the National Mall. It seemed like everyone in the capital was there to pray—there were two large events happening on the same day—The Return and an event hosted by the Graham organization. All of us were there for the same reason, to repent, humble ourselves before God, and pray for our nation.

The Return was the best Solemn Assembly I have had the privilege to be part of—the repentance and prayer were genuine and heart-felt. As I looked out over the crowd of tens of thousands, I had another realization—a much larger group was joining online. As we were gathering in D.C. with tens of thousands, we were leading a much larger prayer meeting with tens of millions of participants.

I spent most of our time there on my face—we were there to repent as a nation, and somehow when I'm fasting, I find myself praying on the ground more than usual. The question from Joel chapter 2 was resonating in my mind, "Who knows?" Who knows how God will respond if we humble ourselves and cry out to Him. Who knows?

Jonathan Cahn gave a keynote message. As I listened to him speak, I noticed a large, clay pot on the stage. I had a suspicion about what the pot was for. In the book of Jeremiah, the prophet breaks a clay pot, symbolizing the Lord removing His covenant blessings from the nation.

Jonathan outlined how since the warning of 9/11 America had repeatedly and persistently rejected and rebelled against God's law and God's ways. At the end of His message, He smashed the pot representing God breaking His covenant of blessing with this nation because of our rebellion. Some people in the audience cheered.

"Don't they know that's a very bad thing?" I said to the person next to me.

But even as Jonathan prophesied judgments on the nation, he also predicted an Acts 2 church emerging into an outpouring of the Spirit in the middle of judgments.

A VERDICT FOR LIFE

We concluded our full day of repentance and prayer at five p.m. Together, we had responded to God as outlined in 2 Chronicles 7:14, in over 120 locations through 10 Days and representing the nation at The Return.

Incredibly, at 5:15 p.m., less than a mile from where we were standing, the White House announced Amy Coney-Barrett as the nominee for the Supreme Court vacancy. Coney-Barrett was known to be the pro-life movement's favorite choice. I knew at that moment we were sitting in the middle of the answered prayers of millions of believers.

Ruth Bader-Ginsberg had died at the start of the 10 Days. Now, just fifteen minutes after a day of fasting and repentance for national sins, she had been replaced with a staunchly pro-life Supreme Court Justice. You don't have to be very spiritual to see the significance, or to realize that God was answering the prayers of His people. While the White House had not hosted 10 Days, God used them to release the biggest answer to prayer of 2020.

Fast-forward to June 2022, and Roe v. Wade, the court case that made killing an unborn child a constitutional right in all fifty states, was overturned fifty years after it was passed. The impossible had happened. God had heard our prayers.

CONCLUSION

As 10 Days concluded, some part of me was disappointed we hadn't seen Seymour's global outpouring in 2020, at least not in a form I could recognize. However, I knew God's timing was perfect.

In the meantime, we had seen tens of thousands of believers join in 10 Days all over the world, a hundred thousand praying together on the National Mall, and tens of millions joining in The Return online.

We had experienced the favor of God to grow in the middle of a global pandemic.

We had seen a "Global Upper Room" with more than 120 locations doing what the first disciples and the Pentecostal Pioneers had done.

We had seen cities stop.

And we had seen God answer our prayers for justice at a national level.

23

GLOBAL MOVEMENT, GLOBAL FAMILY (2021-2022)

FROM AMERICA TO THE NATIONS

AFTER the incredible growth of 10 Days in 2020, I had a candid conversation with the Lord.

"I don't want to presume because you blessed us so greatly in 2020 you will do that every year. Last year was very special, but I will understand if we shrink or hold steady this year."

I had experienced many incredible moments of divine favor in the past only to suffer unexpected losses. I wanted the Lord to know I recognized what had happened was by His grace, not by our works.

The Lord surprised me: "You have my favor, permission, and blessing to grow. This is not your idea; this is My idea."

He emphasized again that He really wants people around the world seeking His face during the Ten Days of Awe. His hand of blessing was extended. He wanted 10 Days to continue to grow and expand.

10 Days was born in the USA, but beginning in 2021, international gatherings began to outpace events in America. That year, we had over 200 events take place around the world. The experience of John 17 Unity was now spreading and multiplying through many nations and many movements.

Critical to the expansion of 10 Days globally was the development of a unique 24/7 house of prayer: the Global Family 24/7 Prayer Room. This online prayer platform has provided an ongoing outlet for united prayer among the nations and made a way for leaders around the world to maintain ongoing relationships throughout the year.

THE STORY OF GLOBAL FAMILY

In 2019, Liz Adleta, the international coordinator for 10 Days, proposed hosting a 10 Days event on Zoom. I was skeptical. I'm a bit of a Luddite, and it seemed far-fetched for a virtual prayer meeting ever to be half as good as an in-person prayer meeting. However, in spite of my reservations, I told Liz I'd support her attempt. As a rule, I believe in saying "yes" to people who have vision.

As we met to discuss this first virtual 10 Days, Jason Hubbard, leader of the International Prayer Connect shared his vision for a 24/7/365 online prayer room where people from around the globe could pray together night and day in the spirit of the Moravians. Maybe our 10 Days on Zoom could be a first step to make that vision possible.

When Jason shared his vision, I felt the presence of God wash over my head, covering the top of my body down to my chest, flowing to my toes, and filling me with joy. I knew the Lord wanted me to help Jason with this.

To be honest, the possibility of helping Jason see his vision fulfilled made me far more excited about our 10 Days Zoom Room. Paradoxically, in the Kingdom, we can get more joy from helping others fulfill their purpose in God than even fulfilling our own.

Hearing Jason, I felt like a businessman when he hears about an investment idea that is sure to make millions of dollars. I knew helping make this "God-idea" come to pass was going to be incredibly profitable in the Kingdom.

AN EXPERIMENT

Our first 24/7 online prayer event in 2019 was an experiment—could people experience God on a Zoom call just as they do in an in-person worship environment?

In 2019, we had five to ten people online at a time, praying continually in many languages. When I heard their testimonies, it was clear they were "10 Days" testimonies. Holy Spirit had poured out a blessing of supernatural love and unity. Moreover, He had moved in each person's life. People had been saved, healed, set free. Signs and miracles were evident. The experiment worked better than we hoped.

After the success of the online 10 Days in 2019, many people were asking us to keep going with 24/7 prayer year-round. As Jason and I both knew from experience, 24/7 prayer is incredibly hard to sustain. Clearly, we were not ready for that kind of commitment.

FROM 10 DAYS TO GLOBAL FAMILY 24/7

A year later, in the fall of 2020, our global online prayer room had grown by a factor of ten. Now, thousands of people were joining in online prayer. More importantly, we now had a global team of humble, gifted, Spirit-led leaders.

Jason and I spoke once again and realized January 2021 was the right time to birth this online prayer room. We settled on the name "Global Family 24/7 Prayer" because of how we had both witnessed a "global family of affection" begin to emerge during the pandemic. More than ever in our lives, both of us were seeing John 17 unity among followers of Jesus from all nations.

I figured I would help Jason get the prayer room off the ground and then step away. To be honest, I still wasn't crazy about praying online.

A friend of mine called me up. "You probably have no idea how significant this online prayer thing is, do you?" he asked.

"No, I guess I don't really understand it."

"God wants worship 'on earth as it is in Heaven,'" he said. "Heavenly worship never stops—it goes on 24/7."

"Yes, I understand that."

He continued, "But it also involves people from every tribe, every language, every people, and every nation. You're making that part of heavenly worship a reality through this global online prayer room. It's something that's never happened before in history."

"Wow, I never thought of that," I said, dumbfounded. Maybe I needed to stop dismissing the idea of online prayer.

GLOBAL FAMILY 24/7 PRAYER

In January 2021, we launched Global Family 24/7 Prayer Room. We divided the week into 168 hours, and 168 different prayer leaders each signed up to lead one hour of prayer per week. Our leaders and participants were from forty nations and almost twenty languages were spoken in the prayer room.

What started off as a year-long experiment in 24/7 virtual prayer has grown into an online hub of continual prayer from many nations that continues to this day. Global Family has also helped spark other online prayer rooms using a similar model.

I continue to lead GFP side-by-side with Jason Hubbard and a "dream team" of humble, sacrificial, skilled leaders.

A FAILED HOUSE OF PRAYER LEADER MAKES GOOD

I consider myself a failed house of prayer leader.

In total, I've been part of starting at least six houses of prayer that no longer exist—I've failed so often I'm not even sure of the exact number. Some ended because God said, "It's time to end it." Others dissolved because of conflict, persecution, or discouragement While starting houses of prayer has always been part of my calling from God and I love making places for God's presence, my track record has been one of failure after failure, some more spectacular than others.

While I call these things failures—and they are—the Lord continually reminds me that with Him, "failures don't fail."

"What you call failure, I memorialize on My mantle," He tells me.

God enjoys our obedient sacrifices to Him. He memorializes the failures we endure trying to please Him. Without a doubt, He is the kindest Father, Boss, and Friend you could ever meet.

After about a month of 24/7 prayer on Global Family, I had a realization: This is already the most successful house of prayer I've ever been a part of. We were sustaining 24/7 prayer with people from forty nations around the world. If GFP had ended after a month, it would have been worth it. Incredibly, and thanks to the partnership of prayer leaders all around the world, it's still going strong.

THE PERSECUTED CHURCH IN PRAYER

In 2022, 10 Days continued to grow. There were 300 gatherings in fifty nations, with 220 gatherings outside of the U.S.

I was amazed by some of the locations on our map: Iraq, Syria, Lybia, Pakistan, Saudi Arabia. We could not list the cities where these prayer meetings were happening because of the danger of persecution many of our brothers and sisters face daily.

Adapting to an underground church context required a change in our models—we couldn't see city-wide prayer events happening among Muslim background believers. That would be suicidal. But we could see small groups of believers meeting together throughout regions, devoting themselves to extraordinary prayer.

10 Days was close to becoming a majority underground church movement.

ABRAHAM'S STORY

As I have met believers from these areas, it has been incredible to hear what God is doing through extraordinary prayer in some of the hardest, darkest places.

One friend from a Muslim majority nation shared his testimony. We'll call him "Abraham."

Living in one of the most difficult, dangerous parts of his nation, Abraham felt oppressed and afraid. His church was small and not growing. He hated his nation and felt alienated from those around him.

When he found out about the online 10 Days in 2019, he decided to really enter in, taking 10 Days off to pray and fast; just him, alone in his home.

At the end of that time, something had changed. Holy Spirit had given him a new courage and boldness, and also a new humility. His mind had changed—no longer was he focused on old resentments, but he was free to dream with God and love others as never before. God was giving him new vision, and pouring His love out on Abraham, changing his heart. The Lord was speaking to him, leading him, guiding him. Suddenly, miracles and answered prayers began to be quite common rather than rare.

Right away, Abraham saw growth in an "above ground" church context. He also began to see fruit "underground" as former Muslims came to Christ, even militant Islamists. While he is allowed to practice Christianity in his nation, converting Muslims is a crime, so he was now taking his life into his hands. And yet, it seemed worth it considering what Jesus had done for him. He was filled with an incredible love for his Muslim neighbors, a love that led him to serve them sacrificially when a massive natural disaster hit his nation. His service and obvious love for people led to favor with government officials, who routinely asked him to pray for them, and even greater growth among the believers.

As the believers began to multiply, prayer also multiplied, as did Aberaham's influence around the nation. He began traveling all over his nation, uniting believers, stirring up prayer gatherings, and planting churches. In 2022, Abraham saw more than thirty 10 Day prayer gatherings in his nation. In 2023, he saw over seventy.

As I listened to his story, it reminded me of my own story. I was timid, afraid, unsure of my faith. And yet, spending long times in prayer had changed me, given me boldness and direction, and made me fruitful. Somehow, the Kingdom is really as simple as this: if we only abide in Jesus, we will bear much fruit. I suppose 10 Days is really that simple, no matter where you live.

24

THE ROAD AHEAD: MOURNING FOR THE RETURN OF JESUS (2023)

DUBAI

IT'S March 2023 and once again I find myself on the road.

Cassi and I are flying to Dubai for the first international 10 Days Summit. Sixty-five of our friends from around the world meet us there. After Dubai, it's off to India for ten days of vision casting in five cities.

It's our first time hosting a Summit outside of the U.S., and our first time meeting many of our friends in person. My main hope is to bring people into a corporate experience of John 17 unity. We know that if we make Jesus the center of our time, the Lord's presence will come and make us one.

As soon as we start to pray, the Lord seems to walk into the room. Everything is different. The King is here.

The now familiar experience of John 17 unity fills the atmosphere and touches each heart. For some of our friends, this is their first time experiencing this supernatural unity. I look around the room and see Africans, Pakistanis, Indians, North and South Americans, Europeans, Middle-Easterners, and East Asians. We are truly a global family of affection, made one by the blood of Jesus. Jesus is getting what He prayed for—a Bride from every tribe, language, and nation. Faith fills our hearts that He will receive the fullness of His prayer, the fullness of what He gave His life to win, and return for a bride without spot or wrinkle.

REFLECTING ON THE ROAD

As I worship at the hotel in Dubai surrounded by my incredible global family, I find myself reflecting once again on the road trip I took alone in 2004.

God called me then to unite His people in prayer.

I remember the words he spoke to me months later:

"Babylon refuses to mourn. But my people will mourn before I return."

I marvel at how far things have come since then. Despite many obstacles, 10 Days has become a global prayer movement. Each fall, we call believers around the world into a time of mourning for the return of Jesus, and each year more locations and more people answer the call.

Since then, more than a thousand 10 Day prayer meetings have been independently organized, impacting millions of lives.

Thousands of individuals have taken vacation time for 10 Days to fast, pray, and repent.

God has been faithful to pour out miracles, signs, wonders, and answered prayers. It would be impossible to record them all.

My childhood dream to have my life look like something out of the Bible has been fulfilled.

As Cassi grabs my hand, I'm amazed that despite all our trials, we are even more in love than when we started, and more committed than ever to following Jesus and loving His people. We also now have six incredible children.

As thankfulness fills my heart, Psalm 126 flashes across my mind.

"The Lord has done great things for us. We are glad."

THE ROAD AHEAD

As I thank the Lord for what He's done, I find myself reflecting on what is yet to come.

After all these years, I still believe we have yet to experience a loud, global revival. While we have experienced many outpourings, I believe there are greater waves of the Spirit yet to come.

We have yet to see cities around the globe stop to repent and worship Jesus. The Lord still longs to see Ninevahs around the globe humble themselves before Him.

10 Days is not yet a normal, annual appointment with God for most of the church.

We have yet to see people from every ethnic group confessing Jesus Christ as Lord, or the Jewish people *en masse* acknowledging their Messiah.

We have yet to see Jesus receive the full answer to His prayer in John 17—"Let them be one."

All these things and more, I am still longing for, still praying for, still working for. I don't know what I will see with my own eyes, or what is for my children and the generations to come. If my past record is any indication, my vision of the future is likely far from perfect. Truly, "We see in part and prophecy in part."

As I look back over the last twenty years, I find one prayer has grown larger year after year.

"Come Lord Jesus."

My heart is aching to see the Kingdom come on earth as it is in heaven.

"Come Lord Jesus."

Abolish sickness, weeping, sin, and death.

"Come Lord Jesus."

Let your people feel the weight of your absence, so they will cry aloud for your presence.

"Come Lord Jesus."

Come as a Bridegroom for your Bride, bringing justice and vindicating those who wait patiently for You.

"Amen, Even so, come, Lord Jesus."

APPENDIX

THE FIRST NORTHFIELD CONFERENCE: A CALL TO BELIEVERS

By Dwight L. Moody

A CONVOCATION FOR PRAYER, and to wait upon the Lord for a new enduement of power from on high, at Northfield, Massachusetts, from September 1 to 10, 1880.

Grateful as all Christians should be, and are, for the revival of interest in the study of God's word manifest in many quarters - and for the increase of personal and consecrated activity on the part of multitudes of laymen and women, there yet remains a profound sense of a still deeper need among us, namely, a fresh enduement of power from on high.

Without the presence of the Holy Spirit, - whose mission it is to convince, convict and convert men, by giving power to the preached word and sanctifying and making potent personal effort for the salvation of men, - the gospel of the blessed God itself may become, in a measure, a dead letter, and all Christian effort nothing more than the energy of the flesh.

It is Christ's presence in the gospel, by the Spirit, that makes it a living seed, and energizes it in the hearts and consciences of those who read and hear it. We may preach and teach the word, but he only can open the hearts of men to receive it; he only can make the word "quick and powerful"—living and full of energy; and it is his presence only in and upon believers which can enable them to do those "mighty works" which he promised they should do when he went away.

Therefore it was at his command that they tarried at Jerusalem, until they were endued with power from on high by the coming of the Holy Spirit; not in them as a living presence (for that they had), but upon them as an anointing power; so that when they preached and testified the gospel, it was, as Paul said of his preaching, "not in word only, but also in power, and in the Holy Ghost, and in much assurance." And therefore "they had favor with all the people, and the Lord added unto the church daily." It is not only more knowledge and personal activity that we need in the ministry and among the laity, but the presence upon us and with us of the Holy Ghost. For he only can take the things of Christ and show them to us and by us to the world. It is, also, only by his presence in us and upon us, sanctifying our lives, that "we commend ourselves to every man's conscience in the sight of God," as living examples and illustrations of the saving and transforming power of the gospel.

Are we not at ease in Zion? Has not the church, both in the ministry and laity, lost that communion with God which is the condition of power with men? Are we not substituting outward appliances for inward life? In vain do we take the ark to battle unless the Lord himself go up with us. In vain is our learning and all our multiplied machinery if the Spirit of God is not present in power in the church. Are we not too much engaged with questions of "mint and anise and cummin," when we should be on our faces mourning over our spiritual poverty, and seeking new power from God with which to do our Master's work among men?

Feeling deeply this great need, and believing that it is in reserve for all who honestly seek it, a gathering is hereby called to meet in Northfield, Massachusetts, from September 1 to 10, inclusive, the object of which is not so much to study the Bible (though the Scriptures will be searched daily for instruction and promises) as for solemn self-consecration, and to plead God's promises, and to wait upon him for a fresh anointing of power from on high.

Not a few of God's chosen servants from our own land and from over the sea will be present to join with us in prayer and council.

All ministers and laymen, and those women who are fellow-helpers and laborers together with us in the kingdom and patience of our Lord Jesus Christ- and, indeed, all Christians who are hungering for intimate fellowship with God, and for power to do his work, -are most cordially invited to assemble with us. Accommodations will be provided for all who may come. The expense of entertainment will in no case exceed one dollar per day. It is desirable that those who purpose meeting with us should send their names in not later than August 20, to insure accommodation.

It is to be hoped that those Christians whose hearts are united with us in desire for this new enduement of power, but who cannot be present in the body, will send us salutation and greeting by letter, that there may be concert of prayer with them throughout the land during these days of waiting.

Notice of intention to be present, and all letters of inquiry and fellowship, should be addressed to D. L. Moody, Northfield, Mass.

REFERENCES

Chapter 2

Grieg, Pete and Roberts, Dave. *Red Moon Rising.* Lake Mary, FL: Relevant Books, 2003.

Chapter 7

Edwards, Jonathan. "Thoughts on the Revival of Religion in New England," in *The Works of Jonathan Edwards, Volume I.* Peabody, MA: Hendrickson Publishers, 2005. Reprinted from the original 1834 edition published in Great Britain.

Heschel, Abraham Joshua. *The Sabbath.* New York, NY: Farrar, Straus, and Giroux, 1951, 1979, 2005.

Chapter 9

For more stories like this please visit www.sentinelgroup.org/documentaries. Their film "Let the Sea Resound" contains many stories from the Fijian revival from that time period.

Chapter 10 and Appendix

Dorsett, Lyle W. *A Passion for Souls: The Life of D.L. Moody.* Chicago, IL: Moody Publishing, 1997.

JOIN THE MOVEMENT

FIND OUT MORE AT

10DAYS.NET

Have questions?
10DaysCommunications@gmail.com

Visit Our Website
www.10Days.net

Check out these other titles by Presence Pioneers Media.

DAVID'S TABERNACLE
by Matthew Lilley

ENJOYING PRAYER
by Matthew Lilley

Available wherever you buy books or at presence pioneers.org

To get updates and discounts on future book releases visit media.presencepioneers.org or scan the QR code below

Made in United States
Orlando, FL
08 November 2023

38688498R00163